Teaching English Through Action

Bertha Segal Cook

TEACHER'S COMMENTS :

"Berty, the results just amaze me.. They eat this stuff up! I never imagined how quickly English could be taught and learned.."

Lorrie Jones

" I have been using <u>Teaching English Through Action</u> in my class.. It is going great! The kids love it and complain when it's time t o stop"

Liz Wolfe

Published by Berty Segal, Inc.
1749 E. Eucalyptus Street
Brea, California, 92821
Email: bertysegal@sbcglobal.net
http://www.tprsource.com

TABLE OF CONTENTS

LESSON PLANS (continued)

INTRODUCTION

Teaching English Through Action is a comprehensive guide of daily lesson plans implementing the Total Physical Response (T.P.R.) approach to English as a Second Language (ESL). It is an excellent tool for teaching beginning and intermediate students of ANY age level.

Total Physical Response (T.P.R.) is basically a right brained approach to second language acquisition. This strategy has been extensively researched and popularized by Dr. James J. Asher, Professor of Psychology at California State University at San Jose. The intent of Dr. Asher's method and of this program is to "pretune the student with a high level of listening skill so that he will have a perceptual readiness to make a graceful, nonstressful transition to speaking the language."[1]

There are ten units which contain the essential vocabulary needed for survival and success in English. Each unit contains:

1. TARGET VOCABULARY -- this is an overview of the words which will be taught *via commands* in the succeeding group of lessons.

2. INDIVIDUAL LESSON PLANS -- a step-by-step detailing of *exactly what commands* are to be presented. T.P.R. is a euphoric experience for both teachers and students, and it is necessary to have very well planned commands at your fingertips in order to remain "in command of the situation." (Pardon the pun.) With these specific directions you will have control as well as enjoyment.

3. REVIEW LESSON -- this is a review of the vocabulary of the entire unit. This lesson should be given *orally*.

4. RECORD OF MASTERY -- there is a Grid for Recording Mastery (or need for further review) with each Review Lesson. It can serve as:

● a small group (pull-out) grid
● a large group (entire class) grid

This provides a record of each student's progress and will be helpful to teachers and resource teachers in reporting to parents, principal, aide, etc.

You will note that vocabulary development is very carefully controlled. There are never more than eight new words or less than four new words per lesson. Each new word appears (inside a command) several times during the first presentation, then again in the following lessons, in the Review Commands and in further lessons and units. There is actually a tremendous amount of drill in *Teaching English Through Action*. What makes the drill unapparent, and therefore not tedious, is that the words are constantly being RECOMBINED in new and different commands. Thus, you can drill ad nauseum and never feel nausea.

---

[1] James J. Asher, *The Total Physical Response Technique of Learning*, Journal of Special Education, Vol. 3, No. 3.

TOTAL PHYSICAL RESPONSE APPROACH -- BASIC PREMISES

The Total Physical Response (TPR) Approach is based on the concept that language acquisition can be greatly accelerated through the use of kinesthetic behavior (body movement). Dr. James J. Asher, Professor of Psychology at California State Universtiy at San Jose, has researched and documented this approach for the past 22 years. It is the most researched second language approach that exists today. Dr. Asher noted in his early work that young children *without schooling* easily comprehend and uttered thousands of sentences, but both high school and college students, under professional teachers, found the process of second language learning a stressful and often unsuccessful experience. Asher presents solid evidence to support his theory that we have been largely unsuccessful in teaching second languages (foreign or English) because we have overlooked natural language learning sequences, which have been successful. The Total Physical Response strategy is based on the model of how children acquire their first language.

In first language acquisition:

1)   *Listening skill is far in advance of speaking skill.* For istance, it is common to observe young children who are not yet able to produce more than one word utterances demonstrate perfect understanding when an adult says "Run to Grandma and give her a kiss." Asher noted that, "as far back as 1935, teams of investigators such a Gessell and Thompson or Buhler and Hetzer have reported that when children learn their first language, listening comprehension of many complex utterances is demonstrated before these children produce *any* intelligible speech."

Asher infers from his observations, "It may be that listening comprehension maps the blueprint for further acquisition of speaking." Dr. Terrence D. Terrell, Department of Spanish and Portuguese Program in Linguistics, University of California, San Diego, heartily agrees. He states, "the listening comprehension skill is basic. The first step for a language learner is to comprehend the essential idea of what is being said to him."[2]

Implication. Understanding the spoken language should be developed in advance of speaking.

2)   "Adults. . .in first language acquisition, manipulate children's physical behavior by a massive number of commands. *The infant becomes ready to talk only after many months of moving in response to gentle directions from adults. . .*" This is nature's model for learning additional languages. Asher continues by stating, "children acquire listening skill in a particular way. . .There is an intimate relationship between language and the child's body."

Implication: "Understanding should be developed through movement of the student's body. The instructor can utter commands to manipulate student behavior. Most of the grammatical structure of the target language and hundreds of vocabulary items can be learned through the skillful use of the imperative by the instructor."

3)   The third element in first language acquisition is: *speech emerges naturally in the first language; it is not forced.* Asher noted that in second language training,

when speech has been forced before the student was ready, the stress that occurred impaired, rather than enhanced, learning. Dr. Stephen Krashen, Department of Linguistics, University of Southern California, has come to the same conclusion. He states his strong support for an early "silent period" in which the student receives comprehensible input, without the stress of having to produce speech. He emphasizes that anxiety strongly affects language acquisition. "The lower the anxiety, the greater the language acquisition. . .For language acquisition, the anxiety level has to be ZERO. Anxiety blocks input."[3]

Implication: "Do not attempt to force speaking from students. As the students internalize. . .the target language through understanding of what is heard, there will be a point of readiness to speak. The individual will spontaneously begin to produce utterances." When speech emerges, it will be imperfect, with many distortions in pronunciation and errors in grammar. The teacher must have patience, accept these errors and strongly limit error correction, knowing that, at the beginning stages of speech production, the most important consideration is COMMUNICATION. Krashen agrees. He states, "Error correction is actually harmful, because it raises the anxiety level." Asher states, "Remember, when the student begins to speak, the individual's entire attention is directed at trying to produce, so the student cannot attend efficiently to feedback from the instructor. This feedback should not interrupt a student in the middle of an attempt to express a thought. . .The feedback should be modified by a wide tolerance for errors. The instructional goal should be uninhibited communication that is intelligible to a native speaker. We want students to talk and talk and talk. Eventually, they can be fine tuned for more perfect speech."

Asher stresses that speech production (expressive stages) is natural, developmental, and a spontaneous reaction that follows internalization (receptive stages -- comprehending) of the target language's 'code'. In other words, the distortions are a necessary aspect of the early stages of speech development and they will be reduced over time, just as errors are reduced, with time, in production of the child's native language.

I would like to add to Dr. Asher's basic statements my own comments based on my experience as both a teacher and a parent.

Reading and Writing -- In first language experience, reading and writing are not required of children until they have had five years of listening experience and at least three years of speaking experience. This implies strongly that it is necessary that we not rush children who are learning a second language into the reading and writing of that language. The natural progression of language acquisition and proficiency is: 1) listening, 2) speaking, and 3) reading and writing.

Implication: We must be careful not to rush students into reading and writing before they have had ample experience with listening and speaking.

In implementing these concepts, this new program provides 102 detailed listening (receptive) lessons and a developmental speaking (expressive) plan. The program removes stress because: (1) the student is required only to respond physically to commands, which most students enjoy doing, and (2) the student is not required to speak until he feels comfortable about expressing himself. Most students begin speaking after approximately 8 to 10 hours of listening (receptive) lessons. IT IS VERY IMPORTANT THAT THE STUDENT BE ALLOWED PLENTY OF TIME FOR THIS RECEPTIVE LEARNING. When the student finally does express him or herself, it has meaning to him/her, and the process has been enjoyable.

REFERENCES

1.   Asher, James J. *Learning Another Language Through Actions, The Complete Teacher's Guidebook.* Sky Oak Productions, Los Gatos, California, 1977.

2.   Terrell, Terrence. Lecture at Santa Ana College at Conference of Orange County Association for Bilingual Ed/English as a Second Language, 1982.

3.   Krashen, Steven. Lecture at Los Angeles County Department of Education and California State University at Fullerton. Krashen, Steven and Terrell, T.D. *The Natural Approach: Language Acquisition in the Classroom.* The Alemany Press, San Francisco, Ca., 1982.

THE METHOD

Rationale

In this program the approach to second language acquisition approximates the pattern of first language acquisition.

1st Language Acquisition

1. Listening (Receptive) -- In first language acquisition, the baby is listening even before birth and continues listening and responding to commands without making any or many sounds himself. We allow the child a great deal of time to listen before expecting speech.

2. Speaking (Expressive) -- Speaking begins between the first and second year. We express great approval when the child produces a "ma ma" or "da da" after months of listening. During this time the child is hearing increasingly complex statements and commands, and decoding and internalizing the sounds.

3. Reading (Receptive learning) and Writing (Expressive) -- These are required only after five years of listening. Teachers please note: We frequently "stampede" to steps 2 and 3 before the limited or non-English speaking student has the opportunity to internalize step 1.

2nd Language Acquisition

1. Listening (Receptive) -- The student finds it easy and pleasurable to learn the 2nd language through commands. Remember that during this 1st step of listening, all sounds are meaningless NOISE or GARBAGE. Very soon the student begins decoding as he/she continues responding physically to commands which are repeated, recombined, and given in "chunks," rather than word by word.

2. Speaking (Expressive) -- Speaking occurs naturally, developmentally, and *without stress* after *approximately* 10 hours of instruction. Students will start chorusing or even yelling the commands. Frequently one student will command another outside the classroom, in line, or on the playground. These are all signs that the student is ready to speak.

3. Reading (Receptive learning) and Writing (Expressive) -- These come easily and naturally after considerable exposure to listening and practice in speaking.

Basic Procedure -- Listening (Receptive) Lesson

Allow a comfortably long receptive stage, and your students' chances of 100% success increase greatly.

1. Demonstration -- Students listen and respond to commands by following the behavior modeled by the instructor.

    Instructor commands and models with

    > 2-3 students

    > entire group

    > 3-4, 4-6 others

    > individual (VOLUNTEER)

2. Instructor commands, without modeling, and

    > group responds

    > groups of 2-3, 4-6 respond

    > individual (VOLUNTEER) responds

3. Instructor combines old and new commands and models with

    > entire group

    > groups of 2-3, 4-6

4. Instructor recombines old and new commands, without modeling, and

    > group(s) respond

    > individual (VOLUNTEER) responds

If there is any hesitance or confusion displayed by students during steps 2 or 4, instructor immediately returns to modeling with them.

NOTE: Keep changing the order of commands. This increases interest.

After APPROXIMATELY 10 - 12 hours on the elementary level, 7 - 9 hours on the secondary level, students will reverse roles with teacher, and command:

> teacher

> other students (small group)

> whole group

> other individual student (VOLUNTEER)

2

The Very First Lesson

The teacher sits on a chair in plain sight of all students. Students should be seated in a semi-circle if possible, so that there is plenty of room for action.

If your students are of limited English speaking capability, you may explain that they will understand perfectly what you are going to say and will know what to do by simply following what you do. If your students are completely non-English speaking, you will not be able to explain. Smile and simply begin.

1.   Sit in front of the room in plain sight of all. Have two chairs on either side of you.

2.   Begin by using hand signals. Motion four students to come up to the front of the group and gesture for them to sit on either side of you, facing the group.

     Say, "stand" and immediately stand up as you motion the students on either side of you to stand up. Then say, "sit" and sit down and motion to the four students to do the same. Repeat this two or three times.

     Then say, "stand" to the entire class and motion them to stand; then "sit" and model and have the group do the same. Repeat several times. Switch to your 'demonstration' group of four students and say, "walk," "sit," and "stand."

     Then say, "walk" to the entire group and model, and the group responds. Then "stop," model, and group responds. Then "sit," "turn," "stop," etc. You're on your way.

     Unit 1 Lesson 1 is an outline description of the lesson you have just read.

Starting with Lesson 2

Spend the firt part of every lesson with the *Review Commands*. Repeat these Review Commands until the hesitation-type movement of students changes to nonhesitation-type movement.

The Commands section provides you with a guided, controlled network of commands. The Novel Commands reinforce vocabulary via humor and serve to test comprehension.

There is no formal "end" to the lesson. Simply congratulate the students with approving statements: "Excellent," "Very good, " "How smart you are!" "Very well done."

Length of a Typical Lesson

The length of a lesson varies greatly, depending on the age and maturity of the students, the size of the group, and the level of language ability.

A general approximation of time is:

- kindergarten and 1st grade students: start with 10 to 15 minutes per lesson; this will soon expand to 20 to 25 minutes.

- 2nd through 6th grades: start with 20 to 30 minutes; this will soon progress to 25 to 35 minutes.

Because the students enjoy the activity, you will find at any age level that their attention span is longer than you anticipated.

- junior and senior high students: 10 to 15 to 20 minute sessions within 45 minutes.

- adults and college students: 15 to 20 minute sessions in one to 2 1/2 hours.

Obviously, in a longer session with older students, you wil be able to cover more than one lesson. A session may include 2, 3, or 4 lessons. (Four is rare.) Do not proceed to the next step until most or all of the students are demonstrating confident (non-hesitating) physical responses to your commands.

Collecting Items -- Props (or Noun Cards)

1. Check existing picture files in your school and or district.

2. Refer to the "Nouns" column on each unit's Target Vocabulary page. It will list which items or picture cards you will need. Items are *preferable* to pictures.

3. Have students, aides, mothers, or anyone help collect these items. Once collected, label and store the items in appropriate Unit boxes (Unit I, Unit II, etc.).

   a. There can be a school Treasure Hunt for these items or pictures of items. "If you can't find it, make it."

   Example: Room 1 -- collects Unit III

   Room 2 -- collects Unit IV

   Room 3 -- collects Unit VI, etc.

   b. Upper grades can make a 5th grade, 6th grade, or simply class project of collecting items as a way of welcoming and helping their new friends.

   c. Jr./Sr. High - period 1 - collects Unit I, II

   period 2 - collects Unit III, IV, V, etc.

   period 3 - collects Unit VI, VII, etc.

General Hints

RESIST THE TEMPTATION TO SPEED THROUGH SEVERAL LESSONS

During T.P.R. sessions, students and teacher frequently become euphoric -- the students because they are aware they are learning quickly, and the teacher because he/she sees such rapid progress. The temptation is to speed through four or five lessons. Resist it. Remember, many repetitions are necessary to insure success.

DO NOT JUMP FROM UNIT TO UNIT

These lessons build up each other. Once you've started in a unit, continue in it. The lessons provide controlled introduction of new vocabulary and a continuous review. Both these elements are necessary for real internalization of the language.

KEEP YOUR COMMANDS "CLEAN"

This means, do only what your command says to do. If, as you command "Jump to the blackboard," you also incidentally scratch your leg, you will see your students responding by jumping to the blackboard and scratching their legs.

COPYING OTHERS IS LEARNING, NOT CHEATING

As students move to the commands, some uncertain ones will turn their eyes to see how their fellow students are moving and will mimic them. This is very acceptable behavior. With T.P.R. students learn by observing others as well as observing the teacher.

INSTANT FEEDBACK

T.P.R. is a very helpful method to the teacher. Because the physical response is so obvious, it tells the teacher immediately what each student comprehends and which commands need repeating.

VOCABULARY IN DIFFERENT REGIONS

As you refer to your nouns list, you may notice that words listed here are different than those used where you live. Feel free to substitute words that are used in your region.

Example: bucket/pail   library/media center

mitt/glove   buggy/carriage

see-saw/teeeter-totter   boots/rubbers

Notes

Notes

SPEAKING

Eliminate stress by allowing students to assume expressive roles *when they are ready*.

Generally, by the time students are into Unit III on the receptive (listening) level, they have begun to demonstrate the wish to be expressive and will express commands they have heard in Units I and II.

Pronunciation

When students first begin to speak, you will notice many errors in pronunciation. Do not attempt to alter these or comment. The student is concentrating so hard on simply speaking, that he's not ready to absorb the finer points of pronunciation. Allow for errors and plan on correcting later when students have a comfortable basic speaking vocabulary. Then say "Yes," and model the statement correctly pronounced.

FROM THIS POINT ON, THE FIRST PART OF EACH LESSON WILL BE THE 1, (2 OR 3) LISTENING LESSONS, AND THE SECOND PART OF EACH LESSON WILL BE THE SPEAKING ACTIVITIES.

THE STUDENT BOOK <u>GENERALLY</u> IS STARTED AFTER THE END OF UNIT III AND CONTINUES ALONG WITH THE SPEAKING STAGES.

SPEAKING (Expressive Stages)

1. **Role Reversal**

    After approximately ten hours of instruction, students and teacher reverse roles and individual students command: a) the instructor, b) other individuals, and c) the whole group. Remember, the students who command *must be volunteers*. The teacher simply asks, "Who wants to be teacher?"

    NOTE: Students commanding teacher -- role reversal

    Keep this relatively short. Young students delight in instructing the teacher to jump, run, skip to the blackboard and turn, etc. They can easily wear you out physically. After four or five commands, have the "teacher" command a small group, the entire group, or one other individual (and "wear them out").

    NOTE: A few of the following examples are taken from Dr. Asher's excellent book, *Learning Another Language Through Actions*.

2. **One-word Response to a Question**

    Start with the imperative. Teacher commands, student responds physically; teacher asks question; student responds.

7

Present Tense

Example A: (An extremely shy student may need the opportunity to simply point.)

"Juan, sit on the chair." (Juan sits)
"Maria, where is Juan?"
(Maria can simply point to Juan.)

"Tom, who is on the chair?"
(Tom can point to Juan and his chair.)

Example B:

Imperative: "Juan, throw the ball to me."
Question: "Who has the ball?"
Response: "Juan."

"Does Maria have the ball?"
"No."
"Does Juan have the ball?"
"Yes."

Example C:

"Pick up one (1) and two (2)."
"Sylvia, give the 1 to Enrique."
"Who has the 1?"
"Enrique."

"Does Sylvia have the 1?"
"No."
"Does Enrique have the 1?"
"Yes."

Example D:

"Maria, put the 5 on the table."
"Is there a 5 on the table?"
"Yes."

"Put the 7 under the table."
"Is the 7 under the table?"
"Yes."

"Is the 5 under the table?"
"No."
(to the class)
"Who has the 5?"
"Maria."

Example E: How Many? (Present Tense)

Introduce "How many _____ do you have?" A short answer is expected.

> "Touch your nose."
> "How many noses do you have?"
> "One."
>
> "Close your eyes."
> "How many eyes do you have?"
> "Two."
>
> "Count the flowers."
> "How many flowers do you have?"
> "Six."

Example F: "Who" questions

(In the following you are providing more opportunities to hear vocabulary review . . . colors, body parts, objects, adjectives, etc.)

> "Look at your friends."
> "Who is wearing a red dress, red socks and black shoes?"
> "Vingh."
> "Who is wearing new blue jeans?"
> "Chang."
> "Who is wearing a striped shirt that is blue and yellow and green?"
> "Arturo."

Example G: Past Tense

> "Betsy, give (throw) me the ball."
> "Who gave (threw) me the ball?"
> "Betsy."

NOTE: With this last example, you've introduced a past tense question, but all that is required is a one-word response.

3.　**Two and Three-Word Responses . . . . Present Progressive Tense.**
　　Levels of questions: (On video tape. . . Refer to page 14)
NOTE: **In questioning students, follow these levels of questions:**

Level 1 -　Who is sitting? Is Juan sitting? Who is tapping his head?
　　　　　(Teacher provides vocabulary; students respond with Yes/No or name (Juan).)

Level 2 -　Is (s)he sitting or standing? Is she tapping her head or her nose?
　　　　　(Teacher provides vocabulary; students respond with verb or a noun.)

Level 3 -　Where is (s)he sitting? What is (s)he tapping?
　　　　　(Teacher provides partial vocabulary; students respond with 3 word phrase "on the chair.")

Level 4 -　What is (s)he doing?
　　　　　(Student provides vocabulary.)

Example A: Present Progressive Tense

"Harry, jump." "Florence, run."
"Who is jumping?" "Harry is."
  (Teacher can add, "Yes, Harry is jumping.")
"Who is running?"
"Florence is."
(Teacher says, "Yes, Florence is running.")
  (By next session, student may say, "Florence is running."

Example B:

"Thieu, sit on the chair."
"Who is sitting on the chair?" "Thieu is."
"Where is he sitting?" "On the chair."
  (Teacher says, "Yes, he's sitting on the chair.")

Example C: "Where" questions

"Put the 6 on the table."
"Where is the 6?" "On the table."
  (It is not necessary for students to respond, "The 6 is on the table."
  "On the table" is adequate.)
"Put the 6 under the 5."
"Where is the 6?" "Under the 5."
"Put the 4 on Sally's feet."
"Where is the 4?" "On Sally's feet."

Example D: Time Telling

Students can make clocks out of paper plates with strong construction paper hands. (Takes ten minutes)

"Set your clock at 6:30," etc.
"It's 9 o'clock." (Students set clocks.)
Then: "Set your clock at 7:30."
    "What time is it?" "It's 7:30."

4. **Short Phrases**

(Teacher touches the table and says)
    "I touch the table."

(Teacher shows continuous motion of touching and says)
    "I'm touching the table." (Present Progressive Tense)
    "I touch my feet." "I am touching my feet."
    "Tim, touch your feet."

(To the class)
    "Tim is touching his feet."
    "Tim, what are you doing?" "What is Tim doing?"
    "I'm touching my feet." "He's touching his feet."
    "Sarah, touch the yellow book."
    "Kim, touch the yellow book that Sarah is touching."
      (longer phrase)
    "Kim, what are you doing?"
    "I'm touching the yellow book that Sara is touching."

Short Phrases (Past Tense)

When students are able to perform the exercises in the present, introduce the past in the same way you introduced the present. (Remember the leveling of questions on p. 10)

    "Henry, throw the flowers on the floor."
    "Pablo, pick up the flowers that Henry threw on the floor."
    "Did Henry throw the flowers?" (Level 1)
    "Did Henry Pick up the flowers?" (Level 1)
    "No."
    "Did Pablo pick up the flowers?" (Level 1)
    "Yes."
    "Where did he throw the flowers?" (Level 3)
    "On the floor."
    "What did Henry do?" (Level 4)
    "(He) threw the flowers."
    "Which flowers?" Level 3)
    "The flowers that Henry threw on the floor."

    "Mary, write your name."
    "Erase the name that Mary wrote."
    "Did you erase the name that Mary wrote?" "Yes." (Level 1)
    "What did Mary do?" "What did you do?" etc. (Level 4)

Short Phrases (Future Tense) (Near, observable future)

Example A:

    "At the count of three, you will stand up."
      (Count or clap hands.)

Example B:

    "I (we) will count (clap) to five. At the count of five, Jan will walk to the door, Maricela will stand on her desk, and Chang will open his book."

"What will Jan do?"
"What will Maricela (Chang) do?"

Example C:

(Using big clock and moving the hands slowly)
"Selma, at exactly 10:30 you will scream."
"What will Selma do?"
"Scream." "She'll scream." "She will scream."
(Move the hands to 10:30, and Selma screams.)

Example D:

"Mark, at 5:15 you will rub your stomach, Steven will scratch his nose and Lydia will close her eyes."
"Will Steven run to the door and open it?" "No."

"Will Lydia scratch her nose?" "No."
"Will Mark rub his stomach?" "Yes."
"What will Mark (Lydia, Steven) do?"

5. **Longer Phrases, Complete Sentences**

"Socorro, tonight you (and Pia) will go to the store and buy a shirt for your father."
(Hold up card reading 'tonight.' Student proceeds through actions. Present progressive or past tense questions can be asked. If 'tonight' concept needs review, hold up a card reading 'tonight' with an identifying night scene...moon and stars, etc.)

"Where are you going tonight?" "We'll go to the store."
"What are you going to do there?" "We'll go shopping."
"What are you going to buy?" "We'll buy a shirt."
"When are you going to go?" "We'll go tonight."

6. **Lists**

"What do you eat in the morning?"
"What do you see in this picture?"
"What will you buy at the market?"

7. **Personal Data**
"Write your first name."
"Write your last name."
"Antonio, write Mr. in front of your first name." etc.
"Read what Antonio wrote."

(Now that the present progressive, past and future tenses have been introduced and practiced often, you can choose which you feel you need to review.)

Example: "What is Antonio writing?"
"What did Antonio write?"
(Before he writes)
"What will Antonio write?"

8. Acting Out States of Being

Students act out feelings and teacher puts words to their actions.

angry	nervous	happy
sad	tired	afraid

Example: "Jose is angry." (Jose frowns.)
"Jose is frowning."
(Jose hunches his shoulders.)
"Jose is hunching his shoulders."
"Jeannette is sad." (Jeannette acts out crying.)
"She is crying."
"She is wiping her eyes."
"She's looking for a Kleenex."
"She's blowing her nose." (She sighs.)
"Thieu is nervous." (Thieu bites his fingernails.)
"He is biting his fingernails." etc.

9. Acting Out Following Reading

By this time students have acquired enough vocabulary to listen to and understand short stories. Procedure for readings, using vocabulary that students are acquainted with:

1) A story is read twice by the teacher. Students listen. Students do not have a copy of the story.

2) The story is read a third time and this time volunteer students act it out. Students wear large name cards of the character they are playing.

3) Students are asked "yes" or "no" and "who, what, where" and "when" questions about the story. Leave out "why" for now.

10. Acting Out Occupations

Divide the class into two or three teams. Students from each team are given the same occupation to act out. The team to guess the occupation first gets the point.

11. Negative

"Pick up two magazines. Put one on the desk and read the other."
"Pick up the magazine that he isn't reading."

13

"Sandy, write your name. Ann, write your name."
"Erase the name that Ann didn't write."

"Pancho Camancho" game (Negative with present progressive tense) (This is a verbal "Hot Potato" game.)
Each student receives one clue card with stick figure depicting an action verb. Start out, "Pancho Camancho isn't washing the window, he's eating." Person with eating card quickly stands up and says, "Pancho Camancho isn't eating, he's dancing." Person with dancing card quickly stands up, and so on.

(Negative and Past Tense) Use appropriate picture cards.

"Pancho Camancho didn't eat a sandwich, he wrote a letter."
"Pancho Camancho didn't write a letter, he read the newspaper."
"Pancho Camancho didn't read the newspaper, he cut the flowers."

12. **More Past Tense** (Integrate several actions)

"Sit on the orange chair."
"Go to the student who sat on the orange chair."
"Cut the paper."
"Throw the paper that he cut."
"Pick up the paper that he threw on the floor."
"John, stand up."
   (Teacher) "He stood up."
"Maria and Rosa, stand up."
   (Teacher states) "They stood up."
"Alicia, stand up, go to the blackboard, write your name, and sit down."
"Alicia stood up, went to the blackboard, wrote her name, went to her chair, and sat down."
Ask "who," "what," "when," "where" questions.

13. **Students Act Out Humorous, Situational Sequences** (NO MEMORIZATION)
Excellent samples of these are in **Live Action English** by Contee Seeley and Libby Romijn. . . . . . Summary of procedure:

   1. Teacher gives situation, modeling with 2-3 students . . . class observes.
   2. Teacher gives situation, modeling and whole class does it.
   3. Class reads the text (from bulletin board) IN CHORUS.
   4. Teacher divides class in groups of 2, students take turns reading lines of the sequence and acting them out.
   5. Students write the lines of the sequence.
   6. Students draw a picture at the end of each line to show they know its meaning.

14. **Students Create Own Dialogues and Act Them Out**

** The <u>levels of questioning</u> (refer back to page 9) are demonstrated in the video tape <u>T.P.R./Natural Approach: the Joy of Language Acquisition</u>   by Berty Segal Cook

TARGET VOCABULARY - UNIT 1

LESSONS 1 - 7

In this unit, you will combine these *ACTIONS* with this vocabulary.

Actions	Nouns	Others
stand	shoulder(s)	your
sit	head	and
walk	ears	my
turn	eyes	to
stop	mouth	up
sing	nose	down
touch	chest	around
smile	arm(s)	the
jump	feet	
point to	leg(s)	
skip	hands	
hop	fingers	
pick up	chair	
put down	table	
put	wall	
	desk	
	door	
	window	
	pencil	
	book	
	ball	
	chalk	

FEEL FREE TO ADD YOUR OWN COMBINATIONS OF THESE ACTIONS AND WORDS. BRANCH OUT! NOVEL COMBINATIONS ARE FUN AND PROVIDE INSTANT FEEDBACK THAT THE ACTIONS AND NOUNS ARE BEING MANIPULATED (DECODED) AND UNDERSTOOD.

UNIT 1   Lesson 1   SELF (BODY ACTIONS)

REVIEW COMMANDS

There is no Review. It is assumed the students know NOTHING.

COMMANDS

Stand

Sit

Walk

Turn

Stop

Sing

(Repeat, and keep changing the order of commands.)

Keep changing the groups commanded. Command groups of 2-3 students, 4-6 others, to the whole group, back to 3-4 others, always in an UNANTICIPATED order. When groups do not know when and if they're "next" to perform, the listening is much keener.

NOTE:

Obviously in a longer session; with older students, you will be able to cover more than one lesson. A session may include 2, 3, or 4 lessons (four is rare). Do not proceed to the next lesson until most or all of the students are demonstrating confident (non-hesitating) physical responses to your commands. However don't proceed too rapidly. Remember, you want this first session to be a complete success.

UNIT 1   Lesson 2   SELF (BODY PARTS)

REVIEW COMMANDS

Stand

Sit

Walk

Turn

Stop

Sing

COMMANDS

Touch your shoulders

Touch your nose

Touch your head

Touch your eye(s)

Touch your ear(s) . . . Sing

Touch your mouth . . . Touch your shoulders

Stand . . . Touch your nose . . . Smile

Sit . . . Touch your mouth . . . Sing

Stand . . . Turn . . . Touch your eyes . . . Smile

Walk . . . Touch your ears . . . Turn

Stop . . . Touch your head . . . Smile

Stand . . . Sit . . . Smile . . . Touch your shoulders

UNIT 1   Lesson 3   SELF (BODY PARTS)

REVIEW COMMANDS

Stand . . . Sit . . . Turn . . . Walk . . . Stop
Touch your head; eyes
Touch your mouth . . . Sing
Touch your nose; ears
Touch your shoulders . . . Smile

COMMANDS

Stand . . . Touch your chest . . . Sit
Touch your feet . . . Walk and smile . . . Jump . . . Stop
Touch your leg(s) . . . Stand
Touch your ears . . . Turn . . . Stop
Touch your hands and your feet . . . Jump . . . Smile
Jump . . . Touch your fingers and your chest
Sit . . . Touch your arms and smile
Touch your head . . . Touch your leg
Touch your shoulders . . . Jump and stop
Touch your chest and your feet

NOVEL COMMANDS

Sit on your hand(s)
Sit on your legs
Walk on your hands and smile

UNIT 1   Lesson 4   SELF - CLASSROOM OBJECTS

REVIEW COMMANDS

Touch your arm(s); finger(s); hand(s)
Touch your head, fingers, hands, and arms
Jump . . . Sit . . . Stand . . . Sing and stop
Walk . . . Turn . . . Stop
Touch your shoulders and your chest

COMMANDS

Touch the wall
Touch the table; chair
Walk to the chair . . . Walk to the wall
Point to the table; chair; wall
Point up and point down
Jump . . . Sit down
Put your head up and down
Put your arms (feet) up and down
Point up to your head
Point down to your feet

NOVEL COMMANDS

Jump to the chair
Jump to the table
Put your head (nose) on the table; chair
Put your chest (ears) on the table; chair
Sit on the table . . . Stand on the table
Put your feet on the wall (NOTE: Let them enjoy this, knowing they can't do it.
Some will try.)
Put the chair on the table and put your fingers on the chair

UNIT 1   Lesson 5   **CLASSROOM OBJECTS**

REVIEW COMMANDS

Touch the table and the chair
Walk to the chair and the table
Point to the table and the wall
Point to (body parts)
Jump to the table
Point down; up
Touch the wall
Touch (body parts)

COMMANDS

Touch my desk . . . Touch your desk
Walk to the window and touch the window
Hop to the table
Hop around the table and point to the table
Sit on the table
Skip to the door; desk; window
Walk around the desk; chair
Point to the window and hop to the door
Walk to my desk and touch my fingers
Jump to the door and stop
Hop to the door (window) and point up; down

NOVEL COMMANDS

Sit on my chair . . . Stand
Jump to the door and hop to the window
Put your (my) chair on my (your) desk
Jump around my (your) chair; desk; table
Put your chest (shoulders) on my chair
Put your leg on the wall
Put your hands on my head
Put my head on your shoulders

NOTE: With Vietnamese students, it is considered disrespectful to touch them
          above the shoulders. Avoid commands which would result in this.

UNIT 1   Lesson 6   CLASSROOM OBJECTS

REVIEW COMMANDS

Touch the table

Walk to the chair; wall; window

Point to my (your) desk; door

Jump around your (my) chair; table; desk

Point to your (body parts that need review)

Skip to the desk and the window

Hop around your (my) desk

COMMANDS

Point to the pencil; chalk

Touch the pencil and the chalk

Pick up the (my, your) pencil; chalk

Pick up the ball and the book

Pick up the chair

Point to the book and the chalk

Point to the ball and smile

Put down the (your) pencil . . . Pick up your book

NOVEL COMMANDS

Put the pencil (ball, book) on your head

Put your nose on the pencil

Put your shoulders on the book

Pick up the book . . . Put the book on your hose and hop to the window

Put the chair on your head . . . Skip around the table

Put down the chair . . . Put the chalk on your toes

UNIT 1   Lesson 7   REVIEW LESSON

This Review Lesson may be used for placement if the teacher feels the student may not need to start with Unit 1. Review lessons, as all other lessons, are to be given orally.

(Review in Unit II)

Stand . . . Touch your head . . . Sing	1.
Jump . . . Touch your shoulders . . . Sit	2.
Touch your eyes . . . Touch your nose	3.
Touch your arms . . . Touch your hands	4.
Stand . . . Touch your fingers . . . Sing . . . Stop	5.
Touch your legs . . . Touch your feet . . . Jump	6.
Touch your chest . . . Turn . . . Stop	7.
Touch your mouth . . . Turn . . . Smile	8.
Turn your head	9.
Touch your ears . . . Walk . . Stop	10.
Jump to the desk	11.
Hop to the window	12.
Skip to the door	13.
Walk to the chair	14.
Point to my chair	15.
Touch the table	16.
Walk around the table	17.
Point up to your nose	18.
Sit down	19.
Touch the pencil	20.
Pick up the ball	21.
Walk to the chalk and point to the chalk	22.
Point to my fingers	23.
Point to the book. . . Touch the book	24.
Pick up the pencil	25.
Put down the pencil	26.
Put my hand on your head (Avoid with Vietnamese)	27.
Put my hand on your shoulder (Avoid with Vietnamese)	28.

UNIT 1 -- Lesson 7

▱ = Presented   ⊠ = Mastered   Date _____

STUDENTS

1																						1
2																						2
3																						3
4																						4
5																						5
6																						6
7																						7
8																						8
9																						9
10																						10
11																						11
12																						12
13																						13
14																						14
15																						15
16																						16
17																						17
18																						18
19																						19
20																						20
21																						21
22																						22
23																						23
24																						24
25																						25
26																						26
27																						27
28																						28

TARGET VOCABULARY - UNIT II

LESSONS 8 - 17

In this unit, you will combine these *ACTIONS* with this vocabulary.

Actions	Nouns	Others
dance	neck	my
frown	hips	on
rub	knees	a
put	stomach	now
write	elbows	me
erase	chin	top of
draw	forehead	bottom of
fold	toes	with
throw	eyebrow(s)	red
catch	cheek(s)	yellow
look at	wrist	blue
show	ankles	green
hit	hair	purple
cut	fingernails	white
color	bell	orange
	pen	brown
	eraser	pink
	name	black
	chalkboard	grey
	paper	big
	notebook	little
	floor	
	bell	
	scissors	

FEEL FREE TO ADD AND MAKE YOUR OWN RECOMBINATIONS

UNIT II   Lesson 8   SELF (BODY PARTS)

REVIEW COMMANDS

(Errors in Review Lesson 7)
Touch the pencil; chair; desk; window
Pick up the ball and the book
Put down the ball
Point to the ball and the chalk
Put down the book and smile
Touch the book and the ball

COMMANDS

Smile . . . Touch your neck
Touch your hips . . . Frown
Touch your neck, turn, and dance
Touch my knee(s) and frown
Now touch your hip(s), sit, stand, smile, and dance
Touch my feet and frown
Touch your knees, smile, and now dance
Now touch my neck, jump, and dance
Touch my feet, walk, stop, dance, and stop
Frown and smile

NOVEL COMMANDS

Walk on your fingers . . . Now stop
Walk on your knees . . . Smile
Now sit on your hands and frown

UNIT II   **Lesson 9**   **SELF (BODY PARTS)**

REVIEW COMMANDS

Frown . . . Dance . . . Stop
Touch your neck and your hips
Touch your hip(s) and dance
Now touch your knee(s), stand, and dance
Touch your chest and frown
Now dance and sing . . . Stop

COMMANDS

Touch your stomach . . . Touch my stomach
Touch your chin and walk to the door
Touch your forehead and smile
Rub your forehead and frown
Touch your toes . . . Touch my toes
Rub your shoulders; neck
Now rub your chin; forehead; toes
Rub your stomach; hands
Touch my fingernail and frown
Touch your elbow and touch my elbow

NOVEL COMMANDS

Rub your shoulders and frown (rubbing hands on shoulders during next commands)
Now rub your shoulders . . . Walk . . . Turn . . . Sit and stand . . . Smile and frown
Sit on your fingers
Rub your forehead on your elbow and frown

UNIT II   Lesson 10   **SELF (BODY PARTS)**

REVIEW COMMANDS

Rub your chin and your stomach
Touch your forehead and your toes
Dance . . . Stop . . . Frown . . . Smile
Touch your fingernail . . . Touch my fingernail
Rub your elbow(s)
Rub (all of the above)

COMMANDS

Touch your eyebrow(s)
Touch your cheek(s) . . . Smile and frown
Rub your cheek(s)
Put your hand on my cheek . . . Stop and dance
Put my hand on your wrist
Touch your ankle
Put my hand on my ankle
Put your hand on your hair
Put my hand on your hair (Avoid with Vietnamese)
Rub your stomach; eyebrow; arm; wrist
Now rub your cheek (knee) and dance
Rub my arm and my wrist
Point to your ankle and touch your ankle

NOVEL COMMANDS

Put your knee on your hand; hair
Put your fingernail on my wrist
Put your elbow on your fingernail and smile
Put your elbows on your eyebrows and frown
Put your forehead on your elbows
Put your wrists on your knees
Put your chin on your shoulders
Put my hand on your toes
Put your elbows on your stomach

UNIT II   Lesson 11   SELF - CLASSROOM OBJECTS

REVIEW COMMANDS

Touch your eyebrows
Rub your cheeks
Point to your wrist
Put your hand on your ankle
Put my hand on my hair
Put your hand on your hair
Rub your eyebrows (cheeks, wrist) and frown

COMMANDS

Walk to the chalkboard . . . Point to the chalkboard . . . Sit
Pick up the pencil; pen; eraser; chalk
Put down the pencil; pen; eraser
Point to the eraser (pencil) and touch the eraser
Write your name
Erase your name
Draw a pen . . . Touch the chalkboard
Point to the eraser . . . Touch the eraser and the chalkboard
Draw a pencil and a book
Erase the pencil and the book
Draw a book
Write your name on the book
Erase your name on the book

NOVEL COMMANDS

Put your feet on the eraser
Sit on the book
Write your name and sit on your name
Put the bell on your hand and dance
Draw a pen and put your head on the pen
Put the pencil on your cheeks
Touch your eyebrows and the eraser and frown
Write your name on your ankle

UNIT II   Lesson 12   CLASSROOM OBJECTS

REVIEW COMMANDS

Pick up the pen ... Put down the pen
Write your name on the chalkboard
Erase your name on the chalkboard
Point to the eraser and the pen
Touch the eraser and the pen; book
Pick up the eraser and the book

COMMANDS

Fold the paper ... Pick up the paper
Throw the paper (eraser, chalk) to me ... Hop to (around) my desk
Pick up the notebook
Skip to the wall ... Walk to the chalkboard
Put the notebook (paper, eraser) on the floor
Walk around the chalk; paper; eraser; pen; book
Hop to the wall; chalkboard
Write your name on your paper ... Erase your name on your paper
Pick up the bell and put the bell on the notebook
Put the notebook and the bell on the floor

NOVEL COMMANDS

Write your name on the eraser; bell; pen
Skip around the notebook ...Put the notebook on your head
Pick up the paper ... Put the paper on your nose
Put your nose on the floor
Put the notebook on the wall ... pick up the notebook
Hop around the bell

UNIT II   Lesson 13   **CLASSROOM OBJECTS**

REVIEW COMMANDS

Fold the paper
Pick up the pencil; pen; bell; eraser; notebook
Skip to the chalkboard; wall; desk; chair
Put the notebook and the paper on the floor
Walk around the table; paper; notebook

COMMANDS

Walk to the chalkboard
Point to the top of the chalkboard
Write your name on the top of the chalkboard
Touch the top of the blackboard
Touch the scissors
Cut the top (bottom) of the paper with your scissors
Show me the top (bottom) of the notebook; paper
Point to the scissors; other classroom objects
Look at the door; scissors; window; table; paper
Hit the door; table; wall
Hit the bottom of your notebook
Hit the top of the chalkboard

NOVEL COMMANDS

Put the bell on your book
Put the book on your head
Hit the wall; pencil; pen; book; scissors
Hit (_____) on the arm
Hit your arm
Hit me on the hand
Hit the scissors with your notebook

UNIT II　　　　Lesson 14　　　CLASSROOM OBJECTS - COLORS

REVIEW COMMANDS

Fold the paper . . . Cut the paper
Cut the bottom of the paper with your scissors
Show me the notebook; (other classroom objects)
Hit the table; wall; door
Point to the door; other classroom objects
Look at the window; other classroom objects
Throw the chalk (ball) to me
Throw (other safe objects) to me; student

COMMANDS

Draw a blue book . . . Touch the blue book
Draw a door . . . Color the door red
Draw scissors
Color the scissors green
Point to the yellow (blue, red, green) paper
Draw a bell . . . Color the bell red; yellow
Draw a table
Rub the red bell and the blue paper
Cut the green paper and fold the green paper

NOVEL COMMANDS

Draw a blue window . . . Draw a red ball around the blue window . . . Cut the
blue window
Put the blue window on your shoulders
Write your name . . . Draw a door around your name . . . Color the door yellow;
blue; green; red
Draw a table on top of your name
Hit your name with a green book . . . Sit on the green book

UNIT II   Lesson 15   **CLASSROOM OBJECTS - COLORS**

REVIEW COMMANDS

Draw a ball and color the ball red
Draw a neck; eyes; body parts
Color the eyes blue and green
Draw elbows . . . Color the elbows yellow
Point to the yellow elbows
Draw a red (green, yellow) table; chair; pencil; book, etc.
Hit the yellow pencil and the green chair

COMMANDS

Fold the white paper . . . Pick up the white paper
Pick up the orange (yellow) paper; book; pencil
Draw a door . . . Color the door brown
Point to the brown book and point to a blue book
Now draw a purple notebook and red scissors

NOVEL COMMANDS

Pick up the white paper . . . Fold the white paper . . . **Put down the white paper** . . . Draw a red chair on the white paper

Draw a purple table under the red chair . . . Sit on the purple table . . . **Stand and smile**

Point to the white paper . . . Draw a brown pencil . . . **Put the paper on your chin**

Walk around the table with the paper on your chin

UNIT II   Lesson 16   CLASSROOM OBJECTS - COLORS

REVIEW COMMANDS

Draw a head . . . Color the head white
Draw hair . . . Color the hair brown
Fold the purple paper
Pick up the orange (blue, green) book
Point to the brown (yellow) pencil
Draw a purple pen; book;/ notebook
Draw a brown eraser and point to the brown eraser

COMMANDS

Throw the grey (pink) box
Pick up the big (little) book
Put down the big book . . . Now put down the little book
Point to the little ball . . . Show me the ball
Show me the black pen
Color the bell (pencil) grey
Fold the grey paper . . . Put it on the pink (black) box
Rub the orange (pink, black) paper and put it on the table
Rub the green box and the yellow pencil
Point to the black eraser and put it on your head

NOVEL COMMANDS

Draw a big box and a little box . . . Put the box on the brown chair and sit on
the box and the chair

Draw a big pink pencil . . . Put your nose on the pink pencil . . . Throw the
pencil to _____

Draw little grey scissors and throw the scissors to _____ . . . Now rub your
big stomach

UNIT II   Lesson 17   **REVIEW LESSON**

(Review in Unit III)

Touch your neck . . . Touch your hips   1.

Sit . . . Touch my chin   2.

Touch your knees . . . Stand   3.

Put my hand on my stomach   4.

Put my hands on your feet   5.

Rub your knees and smile   6.

Put your nose on your hand and frown   7.

Rub your arms   8.

Walk . . . Stop . . . Touch your eyebrows   9.

Turn . . . Stop . . . Touch my elbows   10.

Touch your cheeks . . . Dance   11.

Now walk to the chalkboard   12.

Write your name   13.

Point to your name   14.

Now erase your name   15.

Touch your toes . . . Stand . . . Dance   16.

Touch your fingernails and your hair   17.

Stand . . . Touch your ankles   18.

Now touch your forehead . . . Touch your wrist   19.

Rub your hair   20.

Look at your elbows   21.

Draw a nose   22.

Color the nose pink   23.

Point to the floor   24.

Show me the top of the paper   25.

Write your name on the bottom of the paper   26.

Cut the paper   27.

Fold the white paper   28.

Show me a brown book   29.

UNIT II -- Lesson 17

▱ = Presented   ⊠ = Mastered   Date _____

STUDENTS

	1
1	1
2	2
3	3
4	4
5	5
6	6
7	7
8	8
9	9
10	10
11	11
12	12
13	13
14	14
15	15
16	16
17	17
18	18
19	19
20	20
21	21
22	22
23	23
24	24
25	25
26	26
27	27
28	28
29	29

Test

Point to a yellow pencil	30.
Draw a green chair	31.
Touch the eraser with your scissors	32.
Draw a bell	33.
Show me the big notebook	34.
Hit the floor	35.
Pick up the red ball	36.
Show me the blue eraser	37.
Throw me the little bell	38.
Color the pen grey	39.
Point to the black notebook	40.
Rub the grey scissors	41.

UNIT II -- Lesson 17 Continued

◪ = Presented ☒ = Mastered Date ______________

30																							30
31																							31
32																							32
33																							33
34																							34
35																							35
36																							36
37																							37
38																							38
39																							39
40																							40
41																							41

TARGET VOCABULARY - UNIT III

LESSONS 18 - 31

In this unit, you will combine these *ACTIONS* with this vocabulary.

Actions	Nouns	Others
Turn on	record player	backward
turn off	(phonograph)	forward ·
run	tape recorder	his
push	light(s)	her
pull	box	in
open	flag	it
close	map	under
make	globe	one
shake	ceiling	two
laugh	room	three
get	kindergarten	four
give	blocks	five
knock (on)	doll	six
clap	doll house	seven
count	tea set	eight
add	doll buggy	nine
subtract	dump truck	ten
	wagon	them
	pail	long
	sandbox	short
	teeter totter /	
	(see saw)	
	square(s)	
	triangle(s)	
	rectangle(s)	
	circle(s)	
	rods (sticks)	
	line(s)	
	shelf	rug
	sink	crayons
	cupboard	times
	hook	number

FEEL FREE TO ADD AND MAKE YOUR OWN RECOMBINATIONS. USE THE VOCABULARY INTRODUCED EARLIER. NOVEL COMBINATIONS INTRODUCE HUMOR AND ARE AN EXCELLENT TEST OF COMPREHENSION.

If you do not teach kindergarten, substitute terms of classroom equipment that are RELEVANT to YOUR class.

UNIT III   Lesson 18   CLASSROOM OBJECTS

REVIEW COMMANDS

(Errors in Review Lesson 17)
Throw the big book to _____
Catch the book, _____
Touch the big book with the little book

COMMANDS

Point to the record player; phonograph
Hop to (around) the tape recorder
Walk to the lights and touch the lights
Walk forward
Walk forward and backward
Now hop backward and forward
Turn on (off) the tape recorder
Turn off (on) the record player
Turn on (off) the lights

NOVEL COMMANDS

Throw the red (other color) paper (notebook) on the floor
Throw the book (ball) to Maria
Catch the book (ball), Maria
Throw the pencil to me; Maria; _____
Catch the pencil, Maria; _____; _____
Skip backward
Jump around the desk backward
Point forward . . . Jump forward and point backward
Point to the chalk . . . Walk backward to the chalk

UNIT III   Lesson 19   **CLASSROOM OBJECTS**

REVIEW COMMANDS

Walk backward; forward
Hop forward; backward
Turn off (on) the tape recorder
Turn on (off) the record player
Skip forward
Turn on (off) the lights

COMMANDS

Push his chair forward; backward
Push his book forward; backward
Touch her chair; book; other classroom objects
Point to the box
Run to the wall; chalkboard, etc.
Point to the flag and run to the flag
Touch the big (little) box a (add color words)
Push the big box . . . Pull the big (little) box
Push _____ . . . Pull _____

NOVEL COMMANDS

Run to her chair backward
Push his chair backward . . . Pull her chair forward
Run backward to the flag; chair
Push the box backward
Pull the box forward
Run with her box to the flag and stop

UNIT III   Lesson 20   CLASSROOM OBJECTS

REVIEW COMMANDS

Run to the desk; chair; table; window
Push the chair forward
Touch the flag
Touch her (his) book; pen; notebook
Push his (her) chair forward
Pull his (her) box

COMMANDS

Point to the ceiling . . . Look at the ceiling
Pick up the globe . . . Put down the globe
Close (open) the window
Open (close) the door; book; notebook
Touch the map
Push the map to the globe
Open (close) the box; little blue box; big red box, etc.
Hop around the room
Walk around the room

NOVEL COMMANDS

Open your mouth; eyes; hands
Close your mouth; eyes, hands
Pick up the globe . . . Walk backward with the globe
Hit the globe with the paper
Hit the map with your elbow
Point to the map with your elbow
Push the globe to the window
Touch the ceiling   (Don't worry that this is an impossible command. It is an
                            excellent test of comprehension. Let the students enjoy
                            laughing at the impossibility of it.

UNIT III   Lesson 21   KINDERGARTEN CLASSROOM OBJECTS

REVIEW COMMANDS

Point to the ceiling
Open (close) the door; window; box
Walk around the room
Point to the (class objects which need review)
Push the (class objects which need review)
Pull the (class objects which need review)
Run to the (class objects which need review)

COMMANDS

Walk (hop) to the blocks
Point to the blocks and touch the blocks
Point to the doll; big doll; little doll
Pick up the big doll . . . Put her down
Push the doll to the doll buggy
Push the doll buggy forward
Pull the doll buggy to the blocks
Put the doll in the doll buggy
Point to the playhouse . . . Touch the playhouse
Put the big (little) doll in the playhouse
Point to the tea set . . . Touch the tea set
Pick up the tea set

NOVEL COMMANDS

Put the big (little) doll in the doll buggy; carriage
Put the tea set in the doll buggy
Run with the doll to the playhouse
Put the doll on top of the doll buggy
Run to the tea set and the doll
Rub the doll's head
Rub the doll's head on your head; on (*student's*) head

UNIT III   Lesson 22   KINDERGARTEN CLASSROOM OBJECTS

REVIEW COMMANDS

Put the tea set in the playhouse
Push the doll buggy to _____
Put the doll in the buggy
Push the doll in the doll buggy
Point to the blocks
Run to the blocks
Pick up a big (little) block

COMMANDS

Run to the tricycle
Walk to the tricycle
Walk (skip, hop) to the car and touch the car
Point to the car and frown; smile
Point to the rocking horse
Touch the rocking horse
Sit on the rocking horse
Shake hands
Shake the doll
Shake your head; arms; fingers; lets, etc.
Shake the rocking horse; car
Point to the dump truck . . . Touch the dump truck
Pick up the dump truck

NOVEL COMMANDS

Jump with the doll to the tricycle; car; dump truck
Skip with the doll to the dump truck; car; rocking horse
Put the car on the rocking horse
Shake the doll buggy and run to the playhouse

UNIT III   Lesson 23   KINDERGARTEN OBJECTS

This lesson can be done in the classroom and on the kindergarten playground

REVIEW COMMANDS

Shake your head
Push the car to the dump truck
Push the tricycle around the car
Run with the car to the tricycle
Sit on the rocking horse
Shake hands
Shake hands with me; other students
Pull my hand . . . Push my hand

COMMANDS

Point to the pail . . . Touch the pail . . . Get the pail
Run with the pail to the wagon
Sit on the wagon
Point to the sandbox . . . Walk to the sandbox
Pick up the pail and put it in the sandbox
Look at the teeter/totter . . . Point to the teeter/totter; see/saw
Sit on the teeter/totter and point up and down
Jump to the sandbox and skip to the teeter/totter
Get the wagon and pull it to _____; the table.

NOVEL COMMANDS

Stand on the wagon
Jump backward to the wagon
Shake the wagon and pull it to the window
Push the wagon to the teeter/totter
Get the pail and put it on your head
Put the pail in your mouth and jump
Run and put the pail in the sandbox

UNIT III   Lesson 24   COLORS -- SHAPES

REVIEW COMMANDS

Shake your head; hands
Get the big (little) car; wagon
Get the orange (yellow, other colors) pencil and put it on your paper; desk
Push the car
Pull the car

COMMANDS

Make a square . . . Touch it ., . . Point to it
Make a line . . . Color the line red; other colors
Point to the rectangle and touch it
Make a triangle and a line
Cut the triangle. . . Color the triangle blue
Make a big (little) rectangle . . . Show me the little rectangle
Make a black circle; rectangle; triangle
Make a purple circle and cut it
Make a car . . . Draw a circle around the car

NOVEL COMMANDS

Make a triangle . . . Jump to the wall with your triangle
Cut a rectangle . . . Sit on the rectangle and laugh
Put the big rectangle on your knees; nose
Put the red circle on top of the orange box . . . Skip to the green paper

UNIT III　　　　　　Lesson 25　　　　COLORS -- SHAPES-- NUMBERS

REVIEW COMMANDS

Make a brown rectangle
Draw a black line
Make a big green circle
Make a little orange square and cut it

COMMANDS

Draw one triangle on the chalkboard
Pick up two (one, three) pencils
Pick up four rods; sticks . . . Laugh **and frown**
Put down three rods
Pick up two rods and put one down
Show me three balls . . . Laugh
Draw four rectangles; squares; circles; lines
Show your three squares to (*Jose*)

NOVEL COMMANDS

Put two pencils on one eraser and laugh
Pick up a triangle . . . Put the triangle on *Juana's* head
Draw three little balls on _____ 's forehead
Laugh four laughs
(Add your own zany commands.)

UNIT III   Lesson 26   CLASSROOM OBJECTS -- SHAPES-- NUMBERS

REVIEW COMMANDS

Draw four little tables
Laugh two laughs
Make three balls
Show me one square; circle; triangle; line
Draw four rods
Draw a line and color it orange; other colors

COMMANDS

Point to the shelf; sink
Put a yellow pencil on the shelf
Touch the shelf; sink; cupboard
Put two rods under the sink; shelf; cupboard
Run to the sink; shelf; cupboard
Walk to the shelf and put three circles on the shelf
Put two triangles under the cupboard
Put four rectangles on the sink
Give me three balls and four circles
Put four (three, two, one) squares in (on, under) the cupboard
Give me four circles, two triangles, and three rectangles

NOVEL COMMANDS

Push the balls to *Julio*; other student
Sit under the shelf and laugh
Point to the sink . . . Put three rods in the sink and sit in the sink
(Add some of your own novel commands.)

UNIT III   Lesson 27   CLASSROOM OBJECTS -- COLORS -- NUMBERS

REVIEW COMMANDS

Point to the sink; shelf; cupboard

Give me a box and four rods

Skip to the square; window; door

Put the rods under the shelf; cupboard

Run to the _____ and the _____ and the _____

Give me (classroom objects which need review) ·

COMMANDS

Touch the crayons . . . Show me the crayons

Point to the rug; hook(s)

Give me four crayons . . . Put them on (under) the rug

Knock on the door; wall; floor; window

Knock on four walls

Skip around the rug; classroom objects which need review

Jump to the sink; classroom objects which need review

Walk around the rug; classroom objects which need review

Give me one red crayon and four blue (yellow) crayons

NOVEL COMMANDS

Knock on the table . . . Skip around the table and knock on your head

Put the green crayon in your mouth

Knock on the table with your nose; toes

Run on the rug backwards

Touch the sink and sit on the sink

Stand on the table and point to the hooks; crayons

(Other favorite commands)

UNIT III   Lesson 28   COLORS -- SHAPES -- NUMBERS

REVIEW COMMANDS

Put four rods on the rug
Put three circles under the cupboard
Give me two big circles
Make a big triangle
Put the triangle on (under) the shelf
Knock on the door; window

COMMANDS

Make five triangles and six lines
Make a long line . . . Make a short line
Cut five circles
Make seven rods . . . Color two red and five brown
Make seven squares . . . Pick up five
Clap your hands
Clap to six (five, four, three, two, seven)
Draw a long yellow rectangle
Make six short rods
Show me a long pencil
Show me a short pencil

NOVEL COMMANDS

Cut a triangle . . . Put the triangle on your eye
Pick up six squares . . . Put two squares on your head . . . Put four squares under
your feet and clap your hands

UNIT III　　　　　Lesson 29　　　　COLORS -- SHAPES -- NUMBERS

REVIEW COMMANDS

Clap your hands

Make seven big (little) squares

Cut six circles

Color five squares green

Clap your hands to four; five; six; seven

Draw a long (short) line

(NOTE:　Have a set of number flash cards ready. These are to be used *only* if students understand the *CONCEPT* of the numbers.)

COMMANDS

Count to eight; seven; six; four; two; five; three; one

Show me the number 7; 6; 5; 4; 3, etc.

Clap to nine and give me the number 9

Count to ten . . . Stop . . . Clap to eight

Pick up six circles . . . Add three circles

Count four erasers . . . Add two erasers

Show me eight fingers . . . Add one finger

Add 2 + 3; 4 + 5; 8 + 2, etc.

NOVEL COMMANDS

Pick up the number 5 . . . Show me 5 . . . Put 5 on your nose . . . Throw 5 on the floor . . . Pick up 5 . . . Put 5 and 10 on your chair (Do this with any number.)

Throw 6 to (*student's name*) . . .(*Miguel*), throw the number 8 to *Juan* . . . *Juan*, catch the number 8

Color two fingers red; green

Count to ten . . . Stop . . . Count backwards to one

UNIT III   Lesson 30   COLORS -- SHAPES -- NUMBERS

REVIEW COMMANDS

Show me nine fingers . . . Add one finger
Count to eight; nine; ten
Clap to ten
Show me your eraser
Add four and two
Add three and one

COMMANDS

Count ten rods
Hop nine times . . . Show me the number 9
Show me the green (white, red, yellow) crayon
Jump five times . . . Count to six
Show me the number 1; 2; 3; 4; 5; 6; 7; 8; 9
Count to eight . . . Show me the number 8
Clap to seven . . . Show me the number 7
Subtract one from four (if student has number and subtraction concept)
Subtract three from six
Subtract two from seven

NOVEL COMMANDS

Put the 6 (5, 4, 3, etc.) on your nose
Rub your eraser on the 7; 8; 9; 10
Rub your crayon on your forehead three times; six times; five times
Knock your head nine times and count to nine

UNIT III   **Lesson 31**   **REVIEW LESSON**

(Review in Unit IV)

Turn on the tape recorder   1.
Turn off the lights   2.
Walk forward   3.
Run backward   4.
Touch the record player   5.
Jump to the sink   6.
Open the box   7.
Close the book   8.
Point to the flag   9.
Show me the black crayon   10.
Color the big triangle blue   11.
Cut a green square   12.
Point to the cupboard   13.
Draw a circle green   14.
Walk to the rug   15.
Push the globe   16.
Touch the map   17.
Show me the shelf   18.
Pick up the crayons   19.
Touch the hook   20.
Push the rod with your finger   21.
Jump with the rocking horse   22.
Put the blocks on the table   23.
Push the doll in the doll buggy   24.
Walk to the playhouse with the tea set   25.
Get the wagon and the pail   26.
Show me the sandbox (Teacher will use a picture of this)   27.
Point to the teeter/totter (Use picture)   28.
Shake the dump truck   29.

(Remainder of Lesson 31 is on page 54)

UNIT III -- LESSON 31

▨ = Presented   ⊠ = Mastered   Date _____

STUDENTS

	1	2	3	4	5	6	7	8	9	10	11	12	13	14	15	16	17	18	19	20	21	22	23	24	25	26	27	28	29	
1																														1
2																														2
3																														3
4																														4
5																														5
6																														6
7																														7
8																														8
9																														9
10																														10
11																														11
12																														12
13																														13
14																														14
15																														15
16																														16
17																														17
18																														18
19																														19
20																														20
21																														21
22																														22
23																														23
24																														24
25																														25
26																														26
27																														27
28																														28
29																														29

Test

Lesson 31 Continued

(Review in Unit IV)

Draw a little red rectangle	☐ 30.
Give me two yellow pencils	☐ 31.
Draw five circles	☐ 32.
Make four lines	☐ 33.
Look backward and laugh	☐ 34.
Draw three triangles	☐ 35.
Draw two squares	☐ 36.
Put four crayons under the box	☐ 37.
Put the doll under the doll buggy	☐ 38.
Knock on the door	☐ 39.
Clap to seven	☐ 40.
Show me the number 7	☐ 41.
Count to ten	☐ 42.
Show me eight rods	☐ 43.
Add five and two . . . Add four and three	☐ 44.
Pick up the number 10 . . . Put the 10 on your toes	☐ 45.
Clap ten times	☐ 46.
Subtract five from nine . . . Subtract four from seven	☐ 47.

UNIT III -- LESSON 31 - Continued

☐ = Presented   ⊠ = Mastered   Date _____

STUDENTS

30																				30
31																				31
32																				32
33																				33
34																				34
35																				35
36																				36
37																				37
38																				38
39																				39
40																				40
41																				41
42																				42
43																				43
44																				445
45																				45
46																				46
47																				47

WE LEARN ENGLISH THROUGH ACTION

ABOUT WE LEARN ENGLISH THROUGH ACTION

The Student Book, **We Learn English Through Action** was developed to guarantee that all the material, all the vocabulary covered in the listening lesson plans in **Teaching English Through Action** would later be available to students in an equally organized fashion in speaking, reading and writing activity. IN MOST CASES, on the elementary level, after students have been exposed to the first 3 Units of **Teaching English Through Action**, they will have started their first stage of speaking, Role Reversal; that is, they will have strarted giving the commands to the teacher, to small groups or to individual students. GENERALLY, on the Secondary level, (Jr. and Sr. High School and Adults), Role Reversal will have started by the end of the 2nd Unit. It is then, when students have shown listening comprehension of the material in these first few units of **Teaching English Through Action**, AND when they are giving commands using the same material, that is, in Role Reversal, then they are ready to see and use the material in **We Learn English Through Action**. *From then on the two books can be used together, and the students will ALWAYS BE AT LEAST 2 UNITS AHEAD IN LISTENING COMPREHENSION THAN THEY ARE IN SPEAKING, AND SPEAKING MUST ALWAYS BE AHEAD OF READING AND WRITING.

By following the above rule, the teacher is assured that the student understands EVERYTHING that (s)he is saying, reading, and writing. Another bonus, is that because the student will continually be seeing the words correctly spelled in lesson after lesson, and there is Review built-in each day, the visual impact of this results in much improved spelling. And again, students will only be spelling words they understand and use.

ORGANIZATION AND CONTENTS

The first 10 pages in the Student Book are simple pictures that will provide comprehensible input as to vocabulary meaning, and to provide Humor. Their second purpose is to show students that they can draw simple pictures that can COMMUNICATE MEANING VERY WELL! In fact, page ii is a collection of drawings made by students. Students enjoy drawing to show meaning, and drawing helps retention.

The Units in this student book follow exactly the 10 Units in the Teacher's book of listening comprehension lessons, Teaching English Through Action.

Each Unit is preceeded by a New Vocabulary page. These New Vocabulary pages will be used to develop the student's Picture Dictionary. The size of the pictures in a Picture Dictionary may vary from 3"x3" (or 9 on an 8 1/2x11 sheet) to 2"x2" (or 16 on an 81/2x11 sheet), or simply 1 on each sheet. Specific directions on how to start a Picture Dictionary, and a simple New Vocabulary page will follow, on page 60.

The lessons in each Unit contain ALL the vocabulary on the New Vocabulary page. Review is built-in to every lesson. The new vocabulary is aways esconced inside the Commands, and the Novel Commands provide recombinations of new and old vocabulary. Recombining the different parts, and making sense out of them is a real test of language acquisition. Thus the students are getting Drill, but is drill through humor. The students enjoy the humor, and rarely realize they are being drilled. (Sample lesson, p.61)

The Tests (or Review Lessons) are only in the Teacher's book. A Continuum, of all 10 Tests, has been inserted into the Student book, and it will serve as a record of the student's progress. It will fit exactly into the student's Cum Folder. When the student first gets the book, (s)he should write his or her name on the designated line at the top of the Continuum and return it to the teacher. It can be shown from time-to-time to the students, to administrators, and to parents.
(See sample Test pages and specific directions pp. 64 & 65.)
You may record students' progress on the Continuum Card in Listening, Speaking, Reading, and Writing.

The Student Book is recommended for Grades 3-12, and for adults.

PICTURES, PAGES i-x

p.i. (Unit I) This page is to familiarize students with the written words for the parts of the body. In the listening lessons preceeding this book, all work should have been done using their REAL bodies.

p.ii. (Units 1 and II) This is a simple rearrangement (3 across and 3 down) of drawings done by several students. Pages like this can be used for oral work in class, with the teacher asking what each of the drawings mean. Or particularly humorous drawings may be enlarged, flashed on the Overhead, and oral responses elicited from the students. Later students may read commands and match them to the correct drawings. And even later, have students write what each of the drawings mean.

Students, via their class and homework drawing assignments will be providing you with a continuous supply of the drawings you will need for oral work, reading, (matching), written work, and Testing. Simply copy, cut, and rearrange the drawings, for a variety of multiple choice activities.

*   Teachers have found that using their students' OWN drawings creates a greater sense of ownership, and greater involvement than using prepared drawings. This increased involvement increases the rate of learning and increases retention. Also, students enjoy seeing their drawings in classwork and on tests. There is the double benefit of the humor in their drawings, and their familiarity with the drawings. Both REDUCE THE TENSION OF TEST TAKING.

p. iii (Moods and Emotions) This page works very well with Stage 8, of the Speaking Activities, Acting out States of Being. (p. 12 in the Teacher's Manual). Ennlarge these or the student's pictures showing the various emotions, so that the enlargement is enough to cover the student's entire face. Laminate the picture, so that it is durable. Have students choose an emotion and act it out. Put words to whatever the student "acts out". Thus you will be enlarging the vocabulary of the Emotions.

p.iv (Unit VI) Students may use these pictures along with their own drawings for their Picture Dictionary and for their daily lessons. They may also color the pictures in response to the teacher's oral or written command(s). Make sure to include some outrageous, novel commands along with the "normal" ones ("color the bathroom green"...Harrap's **Communication Games** is an excellent source of humorous pictures.

p.vi (Unit VI) Have students bring REAL household objects from home. Once students have seen these household objects in context, and are aware of their relative size relationship, they can match the pictures to the correct words, and later, "fill-in" the correct words.

p.vii (Unit IX) Bring in large, colorful pictures of animals in their natural habitats and environments. Describe these pictures, with emphasis on the concrete words (color, size, number, etc) and the action taking place.

pp.vii-x (Unit X) Have students bring to class large, colorful pictures or photographs of people at their work in their work outfits or uniforms. Have them bring in identifying samples of their parents' work clothes or equipment. Bring in as much realism as possible to help describe the professions, and make the experience more REAL.

DIRECTIONS TO THE TEACHER
Unit By Unit
(pages noted refer to Teaching English Through Action)

* a new kit, now available, contains all the items needed for all the Units' commands. See p. 59.

Unit I

Make sure that you have collected all the classroom items that are needed, so that students have the necessary materials to follow the commands. (Students can help you collect these items as early homework assignments) The Target Vocabulary List (p.15) will indicate the items needed.

Unit II

Check the Target Vocabulary List (p.24) to see that you (with student's help) have collected all the necessary classroom items.

Unit III

Check the Target Vocabulary List (p.38). Please note that many of these items in this unit are related to the Kindergarden. If you do not teach Kindergarden, CHANGE THESE ITEMS TO FIT WHAT IS RELEVANT TO THE GRADE YOU TEACH.

Unit IV

Check the Target Vocabulary List (p.66). Bring in real articles of clothing. Encourage students to also bring in articles of clothing. Students of all ages enjoy using the actual articles of clothing. The clothing does not need to fit; it's often more fun when the clothes DON'T fit.

You will need to begin to use pictures or photos to illustrate vocabulary. Make sure the pictures are colorful and show size relationship. Appropriate articles of clothing or costumes or masks are helpful.

Unit V

Check Target Vocabulary List (p.82). You may choose to hold (some of) these lessons outside the classroom, or use large picture cards, or large photos of the different parts or personnel of the school. Different schools have different equipment. Use (or substitute) relevant terms only.

Unit VI

Check Target Vocabulary (p.84). You will need many household and yard items. Have students help you bring in as many real items as possible. For the larger items (refrigerator, sink, oven, washer, dryer, etc.) bring in plastic models, colored photos or pictures.

Unit VII

Check Target Vocabulary List (p.112). Gather as many real or plastic fruits and vegetables as you can for these lessons. Use empty cereal, cracker boxes and plastic mustard and ketchup containers with the original labels. Whenever possible, USE REAL ITEMS. They provide more fun, and create greater retention than pictures do. Use plastic representations and pictures when real items are not available.

Unit VIII

Check Target Vocabulary List (p. 124). This Unit reviews classroom objects, colors, numbers, shapes, food, and clothing and introduces the future tense. Be sure to read each lesson carefully, ahead of time, to be prepared with the items you need.

Unit IX

Check Target Vocabulary List (p.138). Past tense phrases are included in commands in this unit. Boehm's Basic Concepts are reviewed in this unit. It will be helpful to have a set of plastic animals and 2-3 sets of colored pictures (preferably pictures which show size relationship) of animals listed in the Nouns column.

Unit X

Check Target Vocabulary List (p.150). Use plastic "dolls" to represent the differnt occupations or ask the students to bring in representative articles of clothing to indicate the occupations. Add ocupations of the students' parents, relatives, and friends, You will also need several musical instruments. As before, use the real items whenever possible.

FOR ALL THE UNITS

Relax and enjoy yourself! Allow for your own and your students' sense of humor. I welcome you to the JOY of Language Acquisition.

Bertha (Berty) Segal

TRANSFER FROM LISTENING ⟶ **SPEAKING** ⟶ **READING** ⟶ **WRITING**
THIS WAS THE TEACHER'S GOAL IN LISTENING COMPREHENSION (LEVEL I) in
Teaching English through Action
IT NOW BECOMES THE FIRST WRITTEN PAGE THE STUDENT SEES IN THE STUDENT
BOOK, **We Learn English through Action.**
*** THE STUDENT BOOK IS BEGUN AFTER:
- Units I, II, and III have been experienced (listening)
    (Units I, II, and III. . . elementary grades)
    (Units I, and II. . . Jr. and Sr. High and Adults)
- The tests for these units have been given and passed (85%)
- Students are giving the commands (1st level of Speaking, Role Reversal)

BEGINNING OF PICTURE DICTIONARY

Teacher announces, "You already know these words. Now let's read them
together.' Teacher points to each word, reads it and acts it out and students mimic,
(in chorus, not individually,) saying the words and acting them out.
Teacher assigns students to draw 5 - 8 - 10 actions, (stick figures) and 5 - 8 - 10 nouns,
(simple COLORED drawings) to show they know the meaning of the word. The
length of the assignment depends on the grade level and ability of the students.

NEW VOCABULARY -- UNIT I

LESSONS 1 - 7

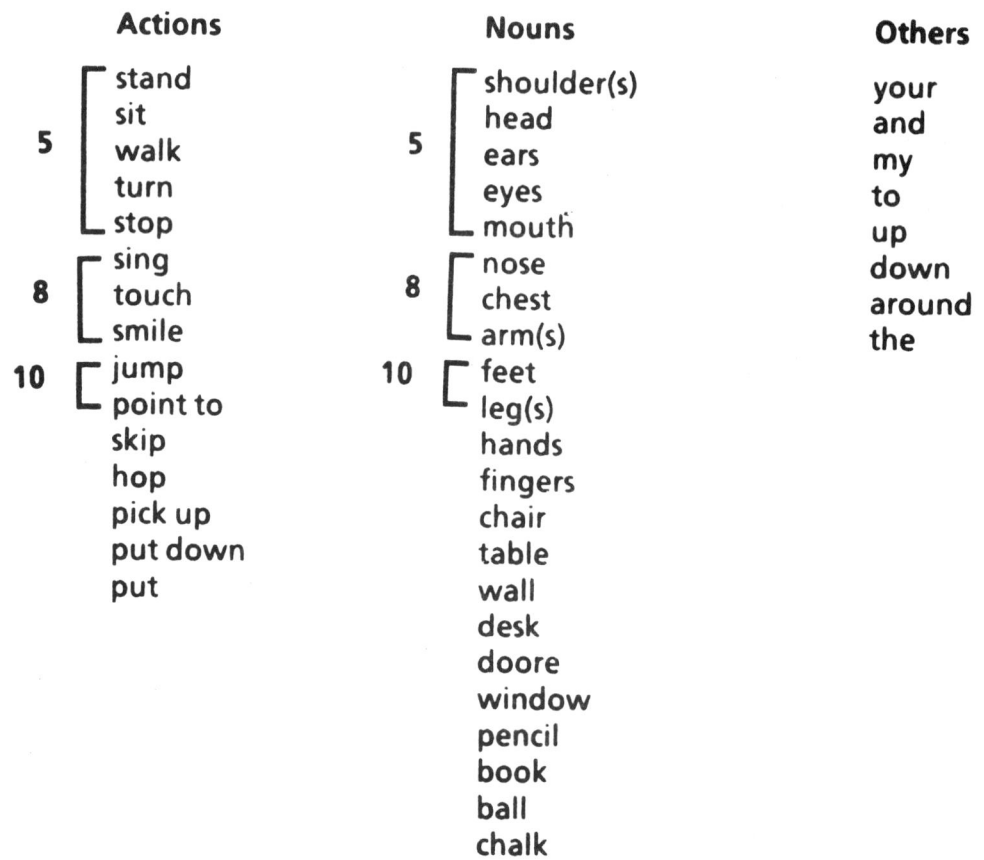

Actions	Nouns	Others
5 ⎡ stand sit walk turn ⎣ stop	5 ⎡ shoulder(s) head ears eyes ⎣ mouth	your and my to up
8 ⎡ sing touch ⎣ smile	8 ⎡ nose chest ⎣ arm(s)	down around the
10 ⎡ jump ⎣ point to skip hop pick up put down put	10 ⎡ feet ⎣ leg(s) hands fingers chair table wall desk doore window pencil book ball chalk	

Note:**   For each Lesson: (This is a sample lesson)

Divide students in groups of 2. Have 1 student give several commands in the lesson to the second student. The second student acts them out. Then they reverse the roles and student 2 gives the commands to student 1 and student 1 acts them out. Or have students alternate: Student 1 gives the commands in the Review section, student 2 gives the commands in the Command section, and student 1 gives the commands in the Novel commands section. Then they reverse roles.

Both of the above activities can be done with groups of 4, with students taking turns being the leader (the one who gives the commands).

Once the oral work is done, have the students copy the whole page of commands and draw stick figures or pictures to show they understand the meaning of the commands. These can be drawn on a separate sheet, labeled ex: "Unit 1, Lesson 4", so that the lesson is clearly identified.

UNIT I   LESSON 4   SELF -- CLASSROOM OBJECTS

REVIEW COMMANDS
>Touch your arm(s); finger(s); hand(s)
>Touch your head, fingers, hands, and arms
>Jump . . . Sit . . . Stand . . . Sing and stop
>Walk . . . Turn . . . Stop
>Touch your shoulders and your chest.

COMMANDS

The drawings they do are copied by the teacher, rearranged 3 or 4 across, and 3 or 4 rows down, made into worksheets or copied onto an Overhead, and they become the basis for
-oral activity in class
-written activity in class
-for homework
-Testing

>Touch the wall
>Touch the table; chair
>Walk to the . . . Walk to the wall
>Point to the table; chair; wall
>Point up and point down
>Jump . . . Sit down
>Put your head up and down
>Put your arms (feet) up and down
>Point up to your head
>Point down to your feet

NOVEL COMMANDS
>Jump to the chair
>Jump to the table
>Put your head (nose) on the table; chair
>Put chest (ears) on the table; chair
>Sit on the table . . . Stand on the table

>Put your feet on the wall. (NOTE: Let them enjoy this, knowing they can't do it. Some will try.)

>Put the chair on the table and put your fingers on the chair

The teacher can use the student workbook in many ways. Here are a number of suggestions that have already worked.

IN THE CLASSROOM
Transfer from Speaking $\longrightarrow$ Writing $\longrightarrow$ Reading

After students have given a number of commands to each other, during the Role Reversal stage, the teacher may say, "We heard some EXCELLENT commands today. Who remembers the command that (Jim) gave? (Jim or another student may supply this.) Teacher says "O.K., you give me that command and I'll write it down." And you follow this procedure:

Student(s) dictate the command.

Teacher writes command on the blackboard or on a large chart-sized sheet.

(ATTENTION SPAN: Take 6-8 commands on the elementary level,

                         10-12 commands on the Junior High level,

                         15-18 commands on the Senior High level.

Students read the commands after all (6, 10, or 15) have been written by the teacher.

Students copy the (6, 8, 10, or 15) commands. This leads to a homework assignment.

HOMEWORK

Ask students to recopy the 6, 8, or 15 commands that were developed and written in class, only now they must be written about 1 1/2 inches apart. In the 1 1/2" space, they are to draw a stick figure shich shows they comprehend the meaning of the command. (These should be drawn with black pencil or ink so they can be copied easily.) These can then be copied by the teacher for use in class with the overhead projector, or for use as a ditto sheet, with 3 figures across, and 3 figures down, so that the ditto sheet contains 9 figures in all. Then they can be used for an oral exercise in class in which the teacher asks, "What does this stick figure mean?" At a later date, these same sheets can be used as a basis for a written exercise, in class, or for future homework.

More Homework Suggestions:

Students collect items, plastic representations, toys, and colored pictures for listening and speaking lessons.

Have students collect pictures or photos which show the meaning of the commands in the lesson.

Cassette tapes - The teacher (or an advanced student) can make a cassette tape of the commands. Have the students take the cassette home, listen to the tape, and act out the commands at home.

TRANSITION TO SPEAKING ----▶ READING ----▶ WRITING ----▶ SPELLING

At the Role Reversal Stage (1st level of speech, when students give commands to others) they are speaking with comprehension.

** <u>What is spoken with comprehension can be read.</u>
<u>What is spoken with comprehension can be written down and read.</u>
<u>Now</u> students transition into seeing/reading/writing the words they speak.

From here on in, ...	<u>General Pattern of the Lesson Plan:</u>
1st 15 minutes...	Listening/Acting Out (Comprehension)
2nd 15 to 25 minutes ...	Speaking Activities (See Speaking Stages. Follow the order presented in this book)
3rd 15-30-45 minutes ...	Picture Dictionary.... Reading and Acting Out.... Writing and Drawing Out Spelling (later... It's O.K. to <u>delay concern about perfect spelling</u>)

<u>The spelling words come from the Target Vocabulary List in each of the Units in this book.</u> (words they understand and use in their speech and reading and writing.) <u>Thus listening, speaking, reading, writing and spelling are related and all based on comprehension!!</u> (In other words, <u>Whole Language</u>.)

TESTING

Knowing in advance what the test items are, (see sample Test of Unit I) the teacher uses the drawings that will be made and handed in by the students as part of their classwork and homework assignments. Choose the most comprehensible and humorous drawings, copy them, and rearrange them in rows of 3 or 4 pictures across, and 3 or 4 pictures down. Give each of them a letter name (a, b, c, d across .. then 2nd line .. a, b, c, d across.) In each line, one of the pictures is the correct item, and the student writes the correct letter on a **separate test sheet.** You will have created a multiple-choice test. Students record the correct letter name, a, b, c, OR d on their test sheet, in repsonse to the teacher's ORAL command.

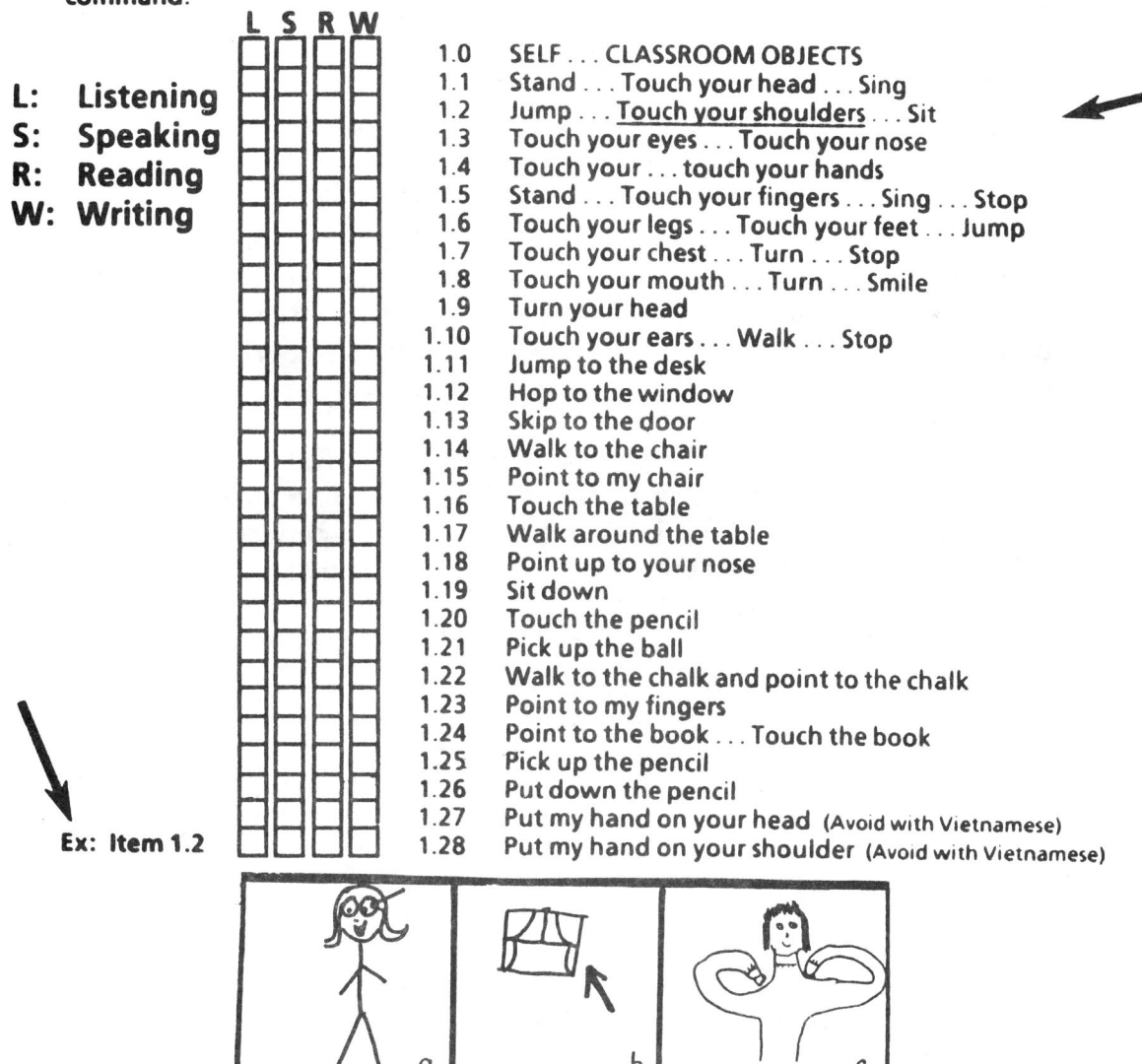

L: Listening
S: Speaking
R: Reading
W: Writing

Ex: Item 1.2

		L S R W	
1.0	SELF . . . CLASSROOM OBJECTS		
1.1	Stand . . . Touch your head . . . Sing		
1.2	Jump . . . <u>Touch your shoulders</u> . . . Sit		
1.3	Touch your eyes . . . Touch your nose		
1.4	Touch your . . . touch your hands		
1.5	Stand . . . Touch your fingers . . . Sing . . . Stop		
1.6	Touch your legs . . . Touch your feet . . . Jump		
1.7	Touch your chest . . . Turn . . . Stop		
1.8	Touch your mouth . . . Turn . . . Smile		
1.9	Turn your head		
1.10	Touch your ears . . . Walk . . . Stop		
1.11	Jump to the desk		
1.12	Hop to the window		
1.13	Skip to the door		
1.14	Walk to the chair		
1.15	Point to my chair		
1.16	Touch the table		
1.17	Walk around the table		
1.18	Point up to your nose		
1.19	Sit down		
1.20	Touch the pencil		
1.21	Pick up the ball		
1.22	Walk to the chalk and point to the chalk		
1.23	Point to my fingers		
1.24	Point to the book . . . Touch the book		
1.25	Pick up the pencil		
1.26	Put down the pencil		
1.27	Put my hand on your head (Avoid with Vietnamese)		
1.28	Put my hand on your shoulder (Avoid with Vietnamese)		

TESTING ------- USING STUDENTS' DRAWINGS

LISTENING-- The entire class is tested at the same time
Tests are multiple choice. Test sheets contain students' pictures, 3-4 across, 3-4 down
Pictures are marked, a.b.c.d.
Teacher gives (reads) the commands orally (out loud)
Students mark (circle) the correct picture.
(Jr./Sr. high, Students may write the correct letter name on a blank sheet of paper.)

SPEAKING-- Students are tested in groups of 4-6
Teacher gathers pictures on individual cards or places them on a large bulletin board, or puts them on transparencies for use with the overhead projector..
Teacher points to pictures, and asks students, "What does this one , that one, mean? (Give each student 2 items at a time)

READING-- The entire class is tested at the same time.
Teacher uses the lst ten items on the test on lst page, 2nd ten items on 2nd page, etc. The ten items are placed on the left hand side of the sheet.
    (See sample, next page)
Students' pictures are placed on the right side of the sheet (make sure to have MORE than 10 pictures) and along the bottom, if necessary.
Students read the items and draw a line from the sentence to the correct picture.

WRITING-- The entire class is tested at the same time.
Test sheets, as in the listening tests, contain lettered pictures, marked. a.b.c.d.,
    3-4 across, and 3-4 down. Students write what each picture means.
Students may write under the picture itself, or on a blank sheet of paper, with the correct letter indicated.
(Teacher may vary the horizontal positions of the pictures, not the vertical positions, in order to prevent copying.)

READING TEST.... 1st PAGE

1.1 Stand..touch your head... sing
1.2 Jump..touch your shoulders.. sit
1.3 Point to your eyes..Touch your nose
1.4 Touch your hips..
1.5 Dance... Touch your mouth
1.6 Sit down and stand up
1.7 Turn...stop.
1.8 Touch your mouth
1.9 Walk to the window
1.10 Point to the window

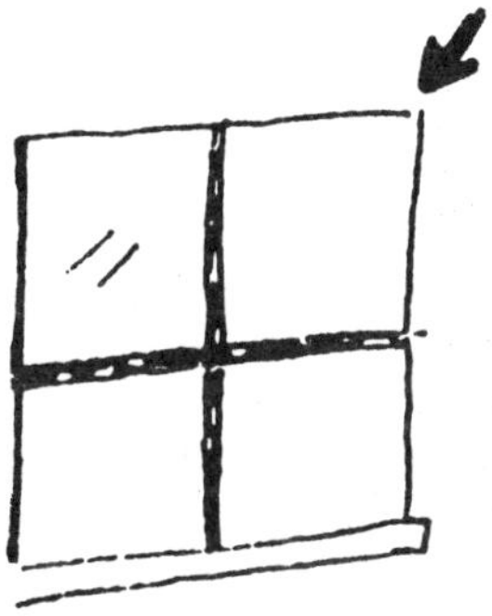

65

TARGET VOCABULARY - UNIT IV

LESSONS 32 - 42

In this unit, you will combine these *ACTIONS* with this vocabulary.
STUDENTS OF ALL AGES ENJOY USING THE ACTUAL ARTICLES OF CLOTHING

Actions	Nouns	Others
pretend	boy	you're
put on	girl	tall
take off	teacher	short
give	librarian	fat
button	nurse	thin
unbutton	man	left
fold	woman	right
tie	principal	next to
zip	secretary	
unzip	custodian	
hang	coat	
hug	shirt	
	blouse	
	jeans	
	hat	
	shoes	
	shirt	
	dress	
	socks	
	boots	
	sweater	
	belt	grandfather
	jacket	bracelet
	ribbon	necklace
	pants	earring
	suit	ring
	pajamas	wrist watch
	baby	bathing suit
	brother	umbrella
	sister	purse
	mother	wallet
	father	apron
	grandmother	overalls

FEEL FREE TO ADD AND MAKE YOUR OWN RECOMBINATIONS. YOU MAY
RECOMBINE WITH VOCABULARY FROM EARLIER UNITS. KEEP USING NOVEL, EVEN
ZANY COMMANDS.

UNIT IV   Lesson 32   SHAPES -- NUMBERS -- SCHOOL PERSONNEL

NOTE: Use real people, or large pictures, or students may "become" these personnel (with appropriate identifying costumes or masks).

REVIEW COMMANDS

(Errors from earlier lessons)
Walk around the circle
Go to the desk
Color the big triangle blue
Color the little square orange
Cut the rectangle
Clap to ten
Add five and three
Subtract six from nine

COMMANDS

Point to a (the) boy
Touch the librarian and smile
Show me the teacher
Touch a girl; boy
Draw a girl (boy) on the chalkboard
Point to the nurse
Show me the librarian
Draw a nurse . . . Color the nurse white
Draw a librarian; teacher; nurse; girl; boy
Walk to the teacher's chair; desk
Pretend you're a nurse (Put nurse's cap or mask on student) . . . Touch my head
Pretend you're the teacher . . . Show me your (the teacher's) desk
Pretend you're a librarian . . . Give me four books

Lesson 32 Continued

NOVEL COMMANDS

Hop around the teacher's desk

Give two triangles and one square to the librarian

Go to (*student's name*), sit on his chair (desk) and frown

Dance around _____'s paper and pencils

Touch the nurse's head with your head

Point to the librarian's feet with your elbow

Put the librarian's books on the teacher's feet

UNIT IV   Lesson 33   SHAPES -- SCHOOL PERSONNEL

REVIEW COMMANDS

Draw a little girl and a big boy
Draw a little teacher and a big nurse
Write your name on the chalkboard
Draw a librarian on three books
Show me the big (little) girl; boy
Point to the little boy
Draw a circle around the girl
Draw a square under the boy

COMMANDS

Show me the principal and point to the principal
Touch the custodian
Point to the secretary and give the secretary a pencil and paper
Point to the man . . . Draw the man on your paper
Touch the woman and point to the woman
Touch the tall woman . . . Touch the short woman
Walk to the chalkboard and draw a woman . . . Now erase the woman
Draw a tall (short) woman; man
Draw a circle around the man . . . Erase the circle
Pretend you're the custodian . . . Give me two balls
Pretend you're the principal
Give the paper to the teacher and give the pencil to the boy
Pretend you're the secretary . . . Show me your papers and pens
Touch the boy on his head; girl on her head
Pretend you're the teacher
Give the chalk (eraser) to the boy; girl
Open the book and close the book
Draw a line on the paper

NOVEL COMMANDS

Skip to the principal and frown
Put the eraser on the secretary's head and smile

(Create some of your own novel commands. Use humor. Don't hesitate to be zany.)

UNIT IV   Lesson 34   SCHOOL PERSONNEL -- CLOTHING

REVIEW COMMANDS

Point to the tall (short) man
Touch the short secretary
Show me the custodian; teacher; principal; librarian
Clap your hands and point to the short girl, boy; man; woman

COMMANDS

Show me the jacket and give me the jacket
Put on the jacket . . . Take off the jacket
Touch the coat
Give the coat to (*student's name*)
Put on the red (other colors) shirt; blouse
Take off the shirt; blouse
Pick up the jeans and put them down
Put on the jacket and take off the shirt
Put the shirt (jacket, coat, jeans) on _____
Give the shirt to me
Give the blouse to me
Put the jeans on the custodian (custodian may be a student or a doll or a picture)
Put the jacket on the principal
Put the coat on the secretary; teacher
Put the blouse on the teacher

NOVEL COMMANDS

Put on _____ 's coat and laugh
Take off your jacket and put it on _____ 's head
Pick up the jeans . . . Put the jeans on your arms . . . Put your arms in the jeans

(It's fun to have a group of students "dress" a student -- over his own clothes.)

70

NOTE: Cover a table with the items (props) named.

REVIEW COMMANDS

Put on the coat and take it off
Give me the jacket
Take off the coat . . . Put the coat on _____
Touch the shirt . . . Put the shirt on _____
Pick up the jeans and put them down
Fold the blouse

COMMANDS

Show me your shoes . . . Tie your shoes
Untie your shoes
Show me the dress . . . Pick up the dress
Draw a dress and color the dress blue; red; yellow
Touch the skirt
Button the skirt; jeans; dress
Pick up the dress . . . Give the dress to _____
Give Juan the shoes and the jeans
Now put the jeans on Kim; other student
Show me the ribbon . . . Tie the ribbon . . . Untie the ribbon
Tie your shoes . . . Tie Thieu 's shoes
Button the jacket . . . Unbutton the jacket

NOVEL COMMANDS

Show me the jeans and put the jeans on _____
Show me the green (other color) ribbon and put the ribbon on (a boy's) head
Put the shoes on your hands and laugh
Pick up the dress and put it on your nose and frown

UNIT IV   Lesson 36   CLOTHING

REVIEW COMMANDS

Show me the orange (other color) dress
Pick up the dress and put it down
Color the skirt red; blue; yellow
Button the dress and unbutton it
Color the shoes black; brown; white
Tie my ribbon . . . Tie my shoes

COMMANDS

Give me the socks . . . Give the socks to _____
Put on the hat and button the jacket
Point to the sweater . . . Color it red
Put on the brown belt . . . Take it off
Push the socks under (on) the table; chair
Show me the boots
Put the boots on (under) the hat; socks; jeans, etc.
Fold the socks; jeans; sweater; blouse
Fold the brown belt . . . Put it on the pink (other color) sweater
Zip the jacket . . . Unzip the jacket; coat
Zip the boots . . . Unzip the boots
Zip the skirt; jeans

NOVEL COMMANDS
Put the (color) socks on _____ 's head; hand
Put the brown belt around _____ 's knees
Put the boots on your arms; the principal's arms
Tie the socks around your shoulders
Put the jeans under the teacher's desk
Put the sweater around the secretary's feet

UNIT IV   Lesson 37   CLOTHING

NOTE: Have a box filled with items named.

REVIEW COMMANDS

Fold the black (other color) dress; belt; ribbon
Put the boots on the table; under the chair
Touch the sweater and put it on
Fold the socks . . . Button the blouse
Give _____ the orange dress
Zip the jacket and unzip it
Put on the sweater . . . Take it off and fold it
Give me the hat

COMMANDS

Open the box . . . Close the box
Point to the pants; raincoat; pajamas
Touch the pajamas and hang them on the hook
Hang the raincoat on the hook
Fold the pants; pajamas
Put the pants in (on, under) the box
Put the pajamas under the pants and the raincoat
Open (close) the box
Zip and unzip (button and unbutton) your raincoat
Touch the umbrella . . . Open the umbrella
Close the umbrella and hang the umbrella on the hook

NOVEL COMMANDS

Hang the raincoat on the chair . . . Tie the pants around the raincoat . . . Point to the pajamas on the table and frown

Hang the pants on the tall man's shoulders
Put the boots under the umbrella

UNIT IV   Lesson 38   CLOTHING -- FAMILY MEMBERS

REVIEW COMMANDS

Hang the raincoat on the hook
Put the pants in the box
Zip and unzip the pants
Button and unbutton the suit
Hang the suit (belt, socks) on the hook
Tie my shoes
Open and close the umbrella

COMMANDS

Touch the baby . . . Touch the baby's head; arms; feet, etc.
Put the baby on the box
Pick up the baby . . . Hug the baby
Pick up the brother . . . Hug the brother
Pick up the sister and the brother and hug the sister
Pickup the tall (short) sister; brother
Hug the fat baby
Point to the thin baby; brother; sister
Put the sweater (coat, jacket, shoes) on the tall (short brother; sister)

NOVEL COMMANDS

Put the baby under the jeans; shoes; socks
Put the brother in the boots; sweater, jacket
Put the shoes on the sister's head and put the sister on the chair . . . Put the baby on the sister

Put the brother under the baby
Pretend you're the sister . . . Hug your fat baby

UNIT IV   Lesson 39   FAMILY MEMBERS

REVIEW COMMANDS

Hug the short brother and the tall, thin sister

Pick up the baby and hug it

Put the fat baby on the chair; table

Put the suit on the brother and the sweater on the sister.

COMMANDS

Show me the father

Touch the mother and point to the mother

Show me the grandmother and pick her up

Point to the grandfather and touch him

Point to the mother and put a dress on the mother

Pretend you're the mother . . . Hug your baby

Pick up the father

Pretend you're the father . . . Put on your shoes and your coat

Put the father next to the mother

Put the grandfather next to the father

Put the fat (tall, short) grandfather next to the thin (tall, short and fat) grandmother

NOVEL COMMANDS

Pick up the baby . . . Put the baby on the mother's head . . . Put the mother on your arms and skip backwards

Pretend you're the father . . . Jump, father, jump . . . Put the boots next to the brother

Pretend you're the mother and jump backward to the father

75

UNIT IV   Lesson 40   CLOTHING

REVIEW COMMANDS

Show me the mother and the father
Point to the sister and the brother
Hug the baby and the grandmother; **grandfather**
Put the mother next to the father
Put the sister next to the grandfather
Put the baby in the mother's arms

COMMANDS

Touch the wristwatch
Put the wristwatch on the father; **grandfather; sister**
Point to the ring
Put the ring on (under) the table
Show me the earring . . . Put the earring on your ear . . . **Put the earring on your**
left ear; right ear
Show me your right (left) arm; leg; foot; **hand**
Touch the necklace
Put the necklace around your neck
Pick up the bracelet . . . Put the bracelet on your right **arm**
Put the bracelet and the necklace on the mother
Pretend you're the grandmother . . . **Put on your earrings and your wristwatch**
(Put different articles of clothing on members of the family.)

NOVEL COMMANDS

Put your wristwatch in your ear
Put the raincoat in the pants
Tie the belt around your head
Hang the necklace on your arms
Put your feet in the box

UNIT IV   Lesson 41   FAMILY MEMBERS

REVIEW COMMANDS

Put the wristwatch in (on, under) the box

Show me the ring

Put the earring on your right ear . . . Point to the necklace

Give me the necklace . . . Give _____ the necklace

Put the bracelet on the sister, mother

Put the bracelet on your left arm

Open (close) my umbrella

COMMANDS

Hang the suit on the hook; chair

Show me the bathing suit

Put the bathing suit on the brother; sister

Fold the bathing suit

Show me the apron . . . Fold the apron

Point to the overalls . . . Pick up the overalls

Put the overalls on the brother; father; grandfather; custodian

Pick up the wallet . . . Put it next to the father

Put the wallet in the overalls; purse

Hang the purse on your right (left) arm

Give me the purse

NOVEL COMMANDS

Pick up the overalls . . . Put on the overalls . . . Put the bathing suit on the overalls

Hang the apron on the bathing suit

Jump around your purse . . . Sit on the purse

Fold your bathing suit and put it on your head . . . Sit next to the principal. Smile

77

UNIT IV   Lesson 42   REVIEW LESSON

(Review in Unit V)

Show me the teacher
Point to the girl; boy
Touch the nurse
Point to the tall boy
Touch the short girl
Show me the principal
Give me the shoes
Unzip the jacket
Button the shirt
Zip the jacket
Fold the blue dress
Put on the blouse
Point to the shirt
Draw the shirt
Color the jeans blue
Put on the hat and take it off
Pick up the ribbon
Touch the skirt
Show me the boots
Give me the belt
Put the socks on the grandfather
Unbutton the sweater and fold it
Fold the raincoat
Show me the black umbrella
Point to the pants
Hang up the white coat
Put the wristwatch on the table
Point to the tall man and pickup the man . . . Put him down
Touch the woman . . . Pick her up and put her down

1.
2.
3.
4.
5.
6.
7.
8.
9.
10.
11.
12.
13.
14.
15.
16.
17.
18.
19.
20.
21.
22.
23.
24.
25.
26.
27.
28.
29.

UNIT IV -- LESSON 42

◨ = Presented   ⊠ = Mastered   Date _____

STUDENTS																							
1																							1
2																							2
3																							3
4																							4
5																							5
6																							6
7																							7
8																							8
9																							9
10																							10
11																							11
12																							12
13																							13
14																							14
15																							15
16																							16
17																							17
18																							18
19																							19
20																							20
21																							21
22																							22
23																							23
24																							24
25																							25
26																							26
27																							27
28																							28
29																							29

Lesson 42 Continued

(Review in Unit V)

Give me the librarian	☐ 30.
Touch the custodian	☐ 31.
Put on the ring and take it off	☐ 32.
Pick up the ring and put it on your finger	☐ 33.
Point to the earring and put it on your left ear	☐ 34.
Put the necklace on the mother	☐ 35.
Point to the bracelet in the box and put it on the sister	☐ 36.
Zip and unzip the overalls	☐ 37.
Pick up the wallet and give it to the father	☐ 38.
Put the purse in the sister's hands	☐ 39.
Put the bathing suit on the brother	☐ 40.
Fold the pajamas	☐ 41.
Tie and untie the apron	☐ 42.
Open the umbrella and close it	☐ 43.
Show me the suit	☐ 44.
Show me the brother and sister	☐ 45.
Pick up the baby	☐ 46.
Put the grandmother next to the mother	☐ 47.
Hug the baby	☐ 48.

UNIT IV -- LESSON 42 Continued

◻ = Presented   ◻⃠ = Mastered   Date _____

STUDENTS																					
30																					30
31																					31
32																					32
33																					33
34																					34
35																					35
36																					36
37																					37
38																					38
39																					39
40																					40
41																					41
42																					42
43																					43
44																					44
45																					45
46																					46
47																					47
48																					48

TARGET VOCABULARY - UNIT V

LESSONS 43 - 50

You will combine these new *ACTIONS* with this new vocabulary.

NOTE: Teacher may choose to hold (some of) these lessons outside the classroom, or use large picture cards, or large photos of the different parts or personnel of the school. Different schools have different equipment. Use (or substitute) relevant terms only.

Actions	Nouns	Others
go to	classroom	in
go in	school	right (Review)
get in (line)	bathroom	left
line up	library/media center	both
drink	office	
hold	flagpole	
hold up	cafeteria	
blow	stage	
blow up	ball	
bring	playground	
	field	
	tree	
	slide	
	bench	
	swings	
	grass	
	bars	
	bicycle	
	bike-rack	
	drinking fountain	
	water	
	bat	
	ball	
	mitt	
	whistle	
	jump rope	
	balloon	

Add and make new recombinations of this and vocabulary from previous units.

In colder regions, you may want to add:

snow	sled	gloves/snow mitts, ear muffs
ice	ice-skates	snow suit

82

UNIT V   Lesson 43   FAMILY AND SCHOOL

REVIEW COMMANDS

(Errors in Review Lesson IV)
Show me the mother and the father
Point to the sister and the brother
Pick up the grandmother
Point to the grandfather
Put the father next to the mother
Put the sister next to the brother
Open (close) the door; box

COMMANDS

Show me the school (actual front of school or large picture)
Walk around the school (students can walk around the picture of the school)
Go to the library (media center) and sit in the library
Point to the classroom and the library
Walk to the bathroom . . . Point to the bathroom
Show the classroom to Maria; Juan, etc.
Show me the office
Open the office door . . . Push the office door
Pull the office door and close it.
Put (appropriate classroom objects or people in appropriate room)

    Example: Put the teacher in the classroom
               Put the books in the library
               Put the principal in the office

NOVEL COMMANDS

Put the pen on (picture of) the library
Sit under the desk in the classroom
Sit under his (her) desk
Put the ball on (picture of) the school
Pull (student) to the library
Push (student) to the bathroom

UNIT V   Lesson 44   SCHOOL

NOTE: The word *hall* is introduced in this lesson. If you have no halls at your
          school, you may choose not to use the word.

REVIEW COMMANDS

Go to the library; office

Point to the office; classroom; bathroom

Go to the classroom

Point to the bathroom and walk to the bathroom

Point to the school (picture)

Put the boy (girl) in the classroom

Put the librarian in the library; media center; hall

Put the father in the office

COMMANDS

Run to the flagpole

Open the office door and point to the principal

Look in the office and point to the secretary

Show me the cafeteria . . . Jump to the stage (if there is one)

Go to the cafeteria

Walk to the media center

Go sit under the flagpole

Stand next to the flagpole

Walk to the office . . . Open the door . . . Go in the office

Look down the hall

Point to the hall

Walk in the hall

NOVEL COMMANDS

Put the scissors on the stage . . . Sit on the stage

Look in the office . . . Put the baby in the office

Put the chair on the playground . . . Stand on the chair

Sit on the stage and smile . . . Frown

Put an eraser at the bottom of the flagpole

Sit in the hall with the teacher; mother; boy; girl, etc.

(Use your imagination for more novel commands.)

UNIT V   Lesson 45   SCHOOL AND PLAYGROUND

REVIEW COMMANDS

Stand next to the flagpole

Walk around the flagpole

Go to the cafeteria, then go in the hall

Point to the hall

Show me the cafeteria

Go to the stage and sit on the stage

Put the principal (teacher, librarian) in the cafeteria; classroom; library

COMMANDS

Skip to the playground . . . Sit on the playground

Walk to the fields and stop

Get in line (or line up)

Walk in line

Girls, get in line (or line up)

Boys, get in line and point to the playground; field

Look at the tree . . . Walk around the tree

Touch the tree and point to it

NOVEL COMMANDS

Hug the librarian

Jump in line to the field

Skip to the field . . . Run to the teacher

Skip in line to the tree and walk around the tree backwards

Push (pull) the tree to the office (Let them "groan" at this impossible command.)

UNIT V   Lesson 46   SCHOOL AND PLAYGROUND

REVIEW COMMANDS

Look at the field; playground
Go to the cafeteria
Walk around the flagpole
Walk backwards to the library
Get in line and walk down the hall
Walk around the playground
Go to the tree and touch the tree

COMMANDS

Go down the slide
Stand on the bench and now sit on it
Go to the swings and point to the tree (if there are trees on the playground)
Sit on the grass and point to the swing; slide; bars
Run to the bars and point to them
Touch the bench two times and walk to the grass; trees
Skip around the tree

NOVEL COMMANDS

Sit on the slide and clap your hands four times
Put your nose on the swing
Go to the bench . . . Stand on the bench and put your hands on your head
Put your head on the bench and frown
Put your elbows on the grass and laugh

UNIT V   Lesson 47   SCHOOL AND PLAYGROUND

REVIEW COMMANDS

Push the swing . . . Pull the swing
Sit on the slide . . . Now go down the slide
Hop to the grass and go to the bench
Touch the bars and skip around the bars
Push the bench to the slides (this may or may not be **possible**)

COMMANDS

Sit under the bars
Hop (go, walk) to the bike-rack
Get in line and walk on the line
Hop around the bicycle
Get the bicycle . . . Pick it up and put it **down**
Walk around the bike-rack
Put the bicycle in the bike-rack and go sit on **the grass**
Go to the drinking fountain . . . Then go to the **grass**
Run to the drinking fountain and drink the water

NOVEL COMMANDS

Push (Maria, etc.) on the swing and frown; laugh; sing
Sit under the bench
Hop backwards to the slide and sit under the slide
Walk on the line backwards
Hop around Lee and knock on his head
Hop around Maria and knock on her head
Jump to the drinking fountain and touch the water . . . **Now shake your hands**
(Other favorite novel commands)

UNIT V   Lesson 48   PLAYGROUND EQUIPMENT

REVIEW COMMANDS

Stand next to the bicycle

Sit on the bicycle

Point to the bike-rack

Walk to the drinking fountain

Drink the water

Point to your right (left) eye; shoulder; arm; foot

Show me the water

COMMANDS

Show me the bat and the ball . . . Give me the bat

Get the ball and hold up the ball

Hold the ball   (this way, students see the difference between "hold" and "hold up"

Put the bat next to the mitt

Put the mitt under the ball

Put the mitt on the bench

Throw the ball to me; (student)

Throw the ball _____ . . . Catch the _____

Throw the mitt next to the ball

Hold the bat; mitt

Hold up the bat; mitt

Hold the ball in (under) the mitt

Put the ball next to the bat

Throw the ball and catch it

Touch the whistle . . . Show me the whistle

Blow the whistle and hold it up

Lesson 48 Continued

NOVEL COMMANDS

Put the mitt and the bat on your head and sit on the ball

Put the bat on your nose and jump backward

Rub the ball on your feet and cry

Blow the whistle . . . Run to the playground and put the mitt
on the swings; slide

Hold up the whistle . . . Put the whistle in your mouth and blow ten times

Hold up your left leg and shake it

Put your left foot in the water and laugh

UNIT V   Lesson 49   **PLAYGROUND EQUIPMENT**

REVIEW COMMANDS

Hop with your right (left) foot
Hold up your right (left) hand
Pick up the mitt . . . Put it down
Throw the ball to (student)
Put the whistle on (in, under) the bench; desk; chair
Hold up the bat . . . Hold the bat
Hold the ball in the mitt
Hold the whistle in your hand
Blow the whistle
Shake Juan's left (right) hand
Hold your right foot in your left hand

COMMANDS

Hold the jump rope
Hold up the jump rope and bring it to me
Jump with the jump rope
Jump to the window (door) with the whistle; (indoor and outdoor equipment)
Pick up the balloon and put it down
Blow the whistle and jump; skip; run
Point to the balloon and touch the balloon
Blow up the balloon
Bring me the jump rope
Bring me the balloon . . . Blow it up and smile
Hold up both arms
Open both eyes and close both eyes

Lesson 49 Continued

NOVEL COMMANDS

Put your right hand on the ball (mitt, jump rope) and hop forwards; backwards

Put your right hand on your right eye and skip backwards

Put your left hand on the bench and sing; laugh; frown

Hold up both arms

Now hold up both feet (Impossible, but let them "realize" this)

Hold up your right foot and your left hand

Open your right eye and close your left eye   (This requires concentration; watch your students *listen* and *think*.)

Now bring me the jump rope; whistle; ball; mitt

UNIT V   Lesson 50   **REVIEW LESSON**

NOTE: This lesson may be conducted outdoors or with the use of large pictures. It may be used as a general placement test. (Delete terms which are not relevant to your school.)

(Review in Unit VI)

Walk to (around) the school	1.
Go to the library; media center	2.
Point to the classroom	3.
Go (walk) to the bathroom (Use picture, please.)	4.
Point to the flagpole	5.
Run to the playground	6.
Walk to the office and go in the office	7.
Go to the flagpole	8.
Skip to (around) the stage	9.
Walk to the field	10.
Walk on the line	11.
Walk to the grass and sit down on the grass	12.
Walk to the library backwards	13.
Touch his (her) bicycle	14.
Throw the ball	15.
Point down the hall	16.
Jump to the playground	17.
Run to the drinking fountain	18.
Sit on the grass	19.
Stand next to the tree	20.
Go to the bench; bars; drinking fountain; swings	21.
Run to the slide	22.
Bring the bicycle to the bike-rack	23.
Sit on the swing and smile; frown; laugh	24.
Put the ball in the mitt	25.
Get the bat and the ball	26.
Hold up both arms and close both eyes	27.
Show me the whistle and the jump rope	28.
Blow up the balloon	29.

UNIT V -- LESSON 50

☐ = Presented   ☒ = Mastered   Date _____

STUDENTS																				
1																				1
2																				2
3																				3
4																				4
5																				5
6																				6
7																				7
8																				8
9																				9
10																				10
11																				11
12																				12
13																				13
14																				14
15																				15
16																				16
17																				17
18																				18
19																				19
20																				20
21																				21
22																				22
23																				23
24																				24
25																				25
26																				26
27																				27
28																				28
29																				29

TARGET VOCABULARY - UNIT VI

LESSONS 51 - 63

You will combine these new *ACTIONS* with this new vocabulary.

Actions	Nouns		Others
flush	bucket	kitchen	wide
wash	iron	refrigerator	narrow
rinse	ironing board	sink	or
dry	washer	oven	into
comb	dryer	range	to the right of
pour	telephone	pitcher	to the left of
	radio	pan	between
	television T.V.	plate	
	sewing machine	bowl	
	waste basket	cup	
	vacuum cleaner	glass	
	broom	spoon	
	dust pan	fork	
	mop	knife	
	living room	napkin	
	couch	house	
	chair	garage	
	lamp	hammer	
	bedroom	shovel	
	dresser	nails	
	bed	ladder	
	closet	yard	
	bathroom	garbage can	
	soap	gate	
	Shower	fence	
	Toilet	rake	
	comb	hose	
	towel		
	washcloth		
	toothbrush		
	hairbrush		

REMEMBER TO ADD YOUR OWN RECOMBINATIONS OF ACTIONS AND VOCABULARY

UNIT VI   Lesson 51   HOUSEHOLD EQUIPMENT & APPLIANCES

REVIEW COMMANDS

(Errors in Review Lesson 50)
Show me the jump rope . . . Jump with the jump rope
Pick up the balloon and blow it up
Bring me both the balloon and the jump rope
Show me two balloons
Blow up both balloons

COMMANDS

Show me the bucket
Touch the iron . . . Point to the iron
Pick up the iron
Touch the ironing board
Put the iron on (under) the ironing board
Hug me; him; her; student's name
Touch the dryer and point to the dryer
Touch the washer
Put the ironing board next to the dryer; washer

NOVEL COMMANDS

Put the bucket in the dryer . . . Jump to the washer
Walk backward to the ironing board
Put the iron in (on) the washer
Pick up the iron and put it under the ironing board
Hug the washer; dryer
Push the bucket next to the washer

UNIT VI   Lesson 52   HOUSEHOLD EQUIPMENT & APPLIANCES

REVIEW COMMANDS

Point to the iron
Show me the ironing board
Touch the dryer
Pick up the bucket and put it down
Touch the washer/dryer
Turn on the washer / dryer
Put the iron on (under) the ironing board
Put the iron next to the bucket

COMMANDS

Show me the telephone . . . Pick it up and put it down
Give me the telephone
Point to the radio
Turn on (off) the radio
Pick up the clock and point to it
Touch the sewing machine
Point to the sewing machine
Give me the wastebasket
Push the clock next to the wastebasket
Put the wastebasket on the sewing machine
Show me the T.V. . . . Put the radio on the T.V.
Turn on (off) the T.V.

NOVEL COMMANDS

Put the clock in the wastebasket . . . Put the wastebasket on the radio . . . Put
the radio on the T. V. . . . Turn on the T. V. and laugh

Put the telephone on the sewing machine . . . Put the sewing machine under
the T. V. . . . Put the radio on your head . . . Turn on the T. V. and laugh and cry

Mario, put the telephone in the wastebasket

Jane, show me the telephone and point to the telephone

UNIT VI   Lesson 53   HOUSEHOLD EQUIPMENT

REVIEW COMMANDS

Touch the iron; ironing board
Show me the telephone
Pick up the wastebasket
Push the sewing machine to the T. V.
Give me the clock
Pick up the radio and turn on (off) the radio; T. V.
Put the radio on the T. V.

COMMANDS

Push the broom; pull the broom
Sweep with the broom
Touch the mop and pick it up
Hold up the broom and the mop
Show me the dust pan
Give me the dust pan
Push the vacuum cleaner and point to it
Give me the broom; mop; vacuum cleaner
Pull the broom to the mop
Push the dust pan to the broom

NOVEL COMMANDS

(Put the different items in (on) other items in the home. Add "laugh" and/or "cry" to particularly silly commands.)

Put the radio and the broom in the bucket
Push the dust pan to the vacuum cleaner
Put the broom and the mop on the T. V.
Put the iron in the dust pan

UNIT VI   Lesson 54   HOUSEHOLD EQUIPMENT -- LIVING ROOM

REVIEW COMMANDS

Point to the broom; dust pan
Push the mop
Give me the broom
Show me the dust pan
Pick up the vacuum cleaner
Sweep with the broom
Sweep (vacuum with the vacuum cleaner)

COMMANDS

Point to the couch . . . Put the radio next to the couch
Turn on (off) the lamp
Put the lamp on the T. V.
Sit on the chair . . . Put the chair next to the couch
Watch (look at) the T. V.
Point to the living room
Maria, walk to the couch . . . Kim, watch Maria walk to the couch
Point to the living room
Put the couch (chair, lamp, vacuum cleaner) in the living room
Sit on the couch in the living room

NOVEL COMMANDS

Put the chair on the couch . . . Sit on the chair
Put the lamp under the T. V.
Put the lamp on your head . . . Point to your head and laugh
Sit on the T. V. (if it's sturdy)

UNIT VI   Lesson 55   HOME -- LIVING ROOM, BEDROOM

REVIEW COMMANDS

Show me the living room
Point to the couch; chair
Sit on the couch; chair
Turn on the radio; T. V. . . . Turn them off
Point to the lamp
Turn on (off) the lamp
Watch the T. V. in the living room
Turn on the T. V., Karen
Georgio, watch Karen turn on the T. V.
Put the mother (father) in the living room

COMMANDS

Point to the bedroom . . . Put the lamp in the bedroom
Show me the bed . . . Put the baby on the bed
Point to the dresser and jump to the dresser
Touch the bed and sit on the bed
Stand next to the bed
Touch the wide bed
Touch the narrow bed
Show me the wide dresser
Show me the narrow dresser
Point to the closet
Open (close) the closet door

NOVEL COMMANDS

Put the lamp under the bed
Put the radio in the closet . . . Point to the closet
Turn on the T. V. and watch it
Put a pencil under the dresser and clap six times
Put (all the above) in the bedroom

NOTE: By this time students should be helping you create zany commands.

UNIT VI   Lesson 56   HOME -- BEDROOM, BATHROOM

REVIEW COMMANDS

Point to the bedroom; living room
Show me the closet
Point to the bed and the dresser
Show me (open, close) the closet door
Point to the wide (narrow) bed
Touch the wide (narrow) dresser
Put the brother in the bedroom

COMMANDS

Walk to the bathroom and point to it
Show me the bathtub
Point to the shower
Turn on the water in the shower
Put the soap next to the shower
Turn on (off) the water
Pick up the soap . . . Touch the soap and put it down
Put the soap in the bathtub
Point to the toilet
Flush the toilet

NOVEL COMMANDS

Pull the broom to the shower and put it under the shower

Push the mop and the bucket to the water . . . Put them on your head and stand in the water.

UNIT VI Lesson 57 HOME -- BATHROOM

REVIEW COMMANDS

Point to the bathroom; living room
Show me the bathroom
Touch the shower and the bathtub
Show me the toilet
Flush the toilet
Put the sister in the bathroom

COMMANDS

Wash your hands (face, neck, arms) with the soap and water
Rinse your hands (face, neck, arms) with the water
Dry your hands with a towel
Sit on the bathtub next to (on) the red (blue) towel
Show me the comb
Put the comb in my (his, her) hand
Touch the green toothbrush
Fold the red (blue, yellow) towel
Put the washcloth next to (on) the towel
Fold the washcloth
Put the hairbrush on (under) the toilet
Sit on the bathtub next to the washcloth
Put the comb on (under) the hairbrush
Brush your hair with the hairbrush
Wash your comb . . . Rinse it and dry it
Now comb your hair . . . Now brush your hair

NOVEL COMMANDS

Sit on the towel (comb, toothbrush, hairbrush) and cry; sing; dance; laugh; frown

Sit under the shower and sing
Put the comb on the toothbrush
Stand on the toilet and point to the toilet

UNIT VI   Lesson 58   HOME -- BATHROOM, KITCHEN

REVIEW COMMANDS

Comb your hair with the comb
Brush your hair with the hairbrush
Give me the comb; hairbrush
Put the toothbrush on the washcloth
Put the washcloth and the soap on the red (green, blue, brown) towel
Put the towel on the bathtub
Wash (rinse) your face; hands; feet; arms; neck, etc.
Dry your face with the towel

COMMANDS

Point to the kitchen
Touch the refrigerator
Open the refrigerator and close it
Touch the sink; T. V.; lamp
Point to the oven . . . Open and close the oven door
Put the lamp on the T. V.
Pretend you're a grandmother (grandfather) . . . Watch T. V.
Turn off the T. V. and cry
Put the (picture of) refrigerator in the kitchen
Put the (picture of) sink next to the refrigerator
Put the oven next to the sink
Show me the range . . . Stand next to the range
Put the (picture of) range next to the stove in the kitchen

NOVEL COMMANDS

Put the lamp in the refrigerator
Put the T. V. in the oven
Sit on the sink and cry
Put the radio on the sink . . . Turn on (off) the water in the sink
Put the toothbrush, towel and washcloth at the bottom of the refrigerator
Put the hairbrush and the soap on top of the refrigerator

UNIT VI   Lesson 59   HOME -- KITCHEN

REVIEW COMMANDS

Show me the kitchen . . . Point to the kitchen
Point to the oven and the range
Touch the refrigerator
Put the soap on (in) the sink
Put the washcloth in the oven
Put the towel under the washcloth
Show me the range
Put the grandmother in the kitchen

COMMANDS

Touch the plate
Put the plate on the sink
Put the pan in the oven
Put the big (little) pan on the range
Show me the big pan . . . Pour water into the pitcher
Pour the water from the pitcher into the glass
Put the glass on the plate; pan
Show me the big (little) bowl; cup
Put the bowl under the plate
Wash (rinse, dry) the bowl and the plate
Dry the plate (glass, cup) with the big towel
Put the pitcher next to the cup; glass; plate; pan

NOVEL COMMANDS

Put the bowl and the pan on the cup
Put the plate on your head and walk forward
Put the glass in the bowl . . . Put your nose in the glass
Put the big pan on your little finger . . . Pick up the pan with your teeth

UNIT VI   Lesson 60   HOME -- KITCHEN

REVIEW COMMANDS

Pour the water into the red (yellow) glass
Show me the blue (white, orange) pitcher
Give me the big (little) plate; bowl
Put the cup in (under) the pan
Put the glass in (next to) the bowl

COMMANDS

Put the spoon on the plate
Put the fork in the cup
Pick up the fork and the spoon . . . Put the spoon to the right of (left of) the fork
Show me the big (little) knife
Fold the wide (narrow) napkin
Put the napkin on the blue plate
Pick up the glass or the plate
Pick up the fork or the spoon
Put down the fork and put it to the left of the knife

NOVEL COMMANDS

Put the spoon in your ear
Put the fork in the bowl . . . Put the bowl under the table
Put the napkin next to the spoon in your ear
Put the pan and the knife in the sink . . . Put the plate under the knife . . . Pick up the pan and the plate . . . Put them in the oven

Jump to the spoon . . . Pick up the spoon and the napkin . . . Put them in the refrigerator and laugh; cry; sing; dance; frown

NOTE: Encourage students to help you create zany commands.

UNIT VI   Lesson 61   GARAGE AND GARAGE EQUIPMENT

REVIEW COMMANDS

Show me the spoon and put it on the plate

Fold the napkin and put it next to the plate

Pick up the cup and the glass and put them down

Put the napkin under the spoon

Put the fork to the left, and put the knife and spoon to the right of it

COMMANDS

Point to the house . . . Show me the top of the house

Touch the bottom of the house

Point to the garage . . . Touch the garage

Pick up the hammer and put it to the right of the garage

Show me the shovel and put it in the garage

Pick up the nail(s) and put them down

Put the nails in a box

Jump (run, skip) to the ladder; shovel; garage; house

Put the ladder to the right (left) of the garage

Push the ladder into the house

Get the father and put him in the garage

Put the dryer in the garage

Put the washer to the left (right) of the dryer

NOVEL COMMANDS

Sit on the hammer

Pick up the shovel and stand on the nails . . . Now sit on the hammer

Jump to the ladder . . . Hop to the dryer . . . Put the shovel on the dryer . . . Put the nails in the washer . . . Point to the nails and jump and laugh

UNIT VI   Lesson 62   GARAGE AND YARD

REVIEW COMMANDS

Point to the house . . . Put the bed and the lamp in the house

Show me the garage

Pick up the shovel; ladder

Put the ladder in the garage

Hit the nail with the hammer

Point to the wide (narrow) box

Put the nails in the box in the garage

COMMANDS

Point to the yard

Show me the garbage can

Put the garbage can in the yard

Draw a garbage can and color it green; brown; yellow

Point to the gate

Draw a gate

Color the gate white; black; grey

Touch the fence

Draw a fence . . . Color the fence brown; green

Point to the rake

Draw a hose . . . Color the hose red; blue; orange; purple

Put the hose in the yard . . . Put the rake next to the hose

Put the rake between the hose and the garbage can

Put the ladder between the gate and the rake; hose

NOVEL COMMANDS

Hit your head with the hammer and cry

Put the garbage can on the fence . . . Put the rake in the garbage can . . . Put the hose next to the rake . . . Sit on the garbage can and point to the yard

Notes

Test

NOTE: This lesson may be conducted outdoors or with the use of large pictures. It may be used as a general placement test. (Delete terms which are not relevant.)

(Review in Unit VII)

Put the iron on the ironing board
Turn on (off) the washer and the dryer
Point to the bucket and pick it up
Point to the T. V. or the radio
Pick up the wastebasket and put it down
Touch the telephone and the sewing machine
Put the comb between the radio and the T. V.
Push the vacuum cleaner
Put the broom under the dustpan
Pull the mop to the broom
Put the mop between the broom and the dustpan
Show me the living room
Put the chair next to the couch
Put the lamp on the table
Touch the bedroom
Push the dresser to the left of the bed
Point to the bathroom
Put the bathtub in the bathroom
Put the soap between the towel and the washcloth
Wash your face with the washcloth (make motions)
Dry your arms with the towel (make motions)
Turn on (off) the water in the shower (make motion of turning)
Point to the toilet and flush it (make motion)
Comb your hair with the comb
Brush your arms with the hairbrush
Brush your teeth with the toothbrush
Put the mop in the kitchen
Put the refrigerator in the kitchen
Touch the refrigerator

1. 2. 3. 4. 5. 6. 7. 8. 9. 10. 11. 12. 13. 14. 15. 16. 17. 18. 19. 20. 21. 22. 23. 24. 25. 26. 27. 28. 29.

(Remainder of Lesson 63 is on page 110)

UNIT VI -- LESSON 63

◨ = Presented   ⊠ = Mastered   Date _____

STUDENTS																					
1																					1
2																					2
3																					3
4																					4
5																					5
6																					6
7																					7
8																					8
9																					9
10																					10
11																					11
12																					12
13																					13
14																					14
15																					15
16																					16
17																					17
18																					18
19																					19
20																					20
21																					21
22																					22
23																					23
24																					24
25																					25
26																					26
27																					27
28																					28
29																					29

Lesson 63 Continued

(Review in Unit VII)

Show me the range and the oven   30.

Put the pan in the oven   31.

Point to the pitcher   32.

Pour water from the pitcher into the glass   33.

Put the pan to the left of the plate   34.

Put the plate under the bowl   35.

Put the cup and the glass on the table   36.

Put the napkin between the spoon and the fork   37.

Give me the knife and the spoon   38.

Put the fork in the glass   39.

Show me the house and the garage   40.

Point to the yard   41.

Put the garbage can in the yard   42.

Put the rake to the right of the gate   43.

Touch the fence and the hose and the rake   44.

Hit the nail with the hammer   45.

Hold up the hammer   46.

Put the shovel to the right of the house   47.

Put the ladder to the left of the garage   48.

UNIT VI -- LESSON 63 Continued

☐ = Presented   ☒ = Mastered   Date _____

STUDENTS

30																			30
31																			31
32																			32
33																			33
34																			34
35																			35
36																			36
37																			37
38																			38
39																			39
40																			40
41																			41
42																			42
43																			43
44																			44
45																			45
46																			46
47																			47
48																			48

TARGET VOCABULARY - UNIT VII

LESSONS 64 - 73

You will combine these new *ACTIONS* with this new vocabulary.

Actions	Nouns		Others
pour	eggs		of
drink	orange juice		some
eat	bread		them
spread	tortillas		
stir	tomato		
pass	lettuce		
	carrot		
	celery		
	salad		
	pumpkin		
	potato		
	corn		
	green beans/beans		
	onions		
	bacon		
	ham		
	chicken		
	hamburger		
	hot dog		
	mustard	cherries	
	ketchup	grapes	
	coke/pepsi	lemon	
	french fries	peach	
	soup	crackers	
	sandwich	banana	
	peanut butter	apple	
	jam/jelly	strawberry	
	rice	oranges	
	butter	pear	

NOTE: Gather as many plastic or real fruits and vegetables as you can for these lessons. Use empty cereal, cracker boxes, and plastic mustard and ketchup containers with the original labels. *Whenever possible, use the real items.* They provide more fun and are less confusing than pictures. Pictures can be used later.

MAKE AND ADD YOUR OWN RECOMBINATIONS. REMEMBER UNUSUAL COMMANDS ARE AN EXCELLENT TEST OF COMPREHENSION.

UNIT VII   Lesson 64   BREAKFAST FOODS

REVIEW COMMANDS

(Errors in Review Lesson 63)
Show me the garbage can
Put the baby (mother, father) next to the garbage can
Point to the hose   . . Put the brother to the left of the hose
Draw a fence and a rake
Color the fence brown and the rake black

COMMANDS

Show me the little (big) eggs . . . Count six eggs
Give (Sal) the milk . . . (Sal), pour the milk into the pitcher
Touch the orange juice
Pour the orange juice into a glass; pitcher; cup
Point to the bread; tortillas
Give me the bread and a glass of milk; orange juice
Point to the cereal
Drink the orange juice
Get the cereal and put it on the table
Drink the milk
Eat the bread; tortillas
Pour the milk into the cereal
Eat the cereal and drink the milk

NOVEL COMMANDS

Pour the orange juice into the milk . . . Drink the milk and the orange juice
Get the cereal and sit under the table . . . Put the cereal under your knees
Put the tortillas on your head and walk backward

UNIT VII   Lesson 65   BREAKFAST FOODS -- VEGETABLES

REVIEW COMMANDS

Drink the orange juice
Pour the milk into the pitcher; glass
Pour the juice into my glass; cup; sink; pitcher
Put the eggs on the table . . . Give them to me
Push the bread to the cereal
Pick up the bread and eat it.

COMMANDS

Show me the lettuce and pick it up
Show me the red (green) tomato
Put the lettuce next to the carrots
Put the long (short) carrot on the table
Put the fat (thin) carrot under the·table
Cut the celery and put it in the box
Maria, pretend you're the mother and cut the carrots and the celery
Now make a salad of tomato, lettuce, carrots and celery
Olmedo, pretend you're the father and eat the salad

NOVEL COMMANDS

Pick up the salad and put it on (under) your chair
Get the carrots and put them on my feet
Throw the celery to (student's name)
Skip to the tomato . . . Put it on Jim's head . . . Point to Jim and laugh

UNIT VII   Lesson 66   VEGETABLES

REVIEW COMMANDS

Cut three tomatoes
Give me three tomatoes and two carrots
Put the tomatoes, lettuce, and celery on the table
Cut the carrots and the celery and put them in the salad
Draw a big (little) green salad

COMMANDS

Show me a big orange pumpkin
Give me the big (little) potato
Put the yellow corn next to the brown potato
Throw the green bean under the table
Put the pumpkin next to the onion
Cut the beans and put them with the onions in a salad
Eat the salad

NOVEL COMMANDS

Throw me a green bean . . . Throw two green beans to Jim . . . Run around Jim, (Maria) and give him (her) a potato and some corn

Put two potatoes on your head and jump to _____
Put two onions on your knees and smile; frown; laugh; sing; dance
Draw some beans and color them purple, black, and orange

UNIT VII   Lesson 67   VEGETABLES -- MEATS

NOTE: A pretend "refrigerator" (open box) to hold the meats makes this lesson
         more fun.

REVIEW COMMANDS

Give the pumpkin and the onion to me; (student)

Put the potato and the pumpkin on (next to) the onions

Cut a potato and give it to _____

Draw a pumpkin and erase it

Cut some beans

Draw some beans and color them brown

COMMANDS

Point to the bacon and put it in the refrigerator

Take the bacon out of the refrigerator

Now put the bacon on the table; sink

Point to the ham (chicken) in the refrigerator

Show me the chicken . . . Touch the ham and eat the bacon

Put the hamburger under (on top of) the bacon

Pick up the hot dog and the tortilla and eat them

Put the hot dog in the tortilla (bun) and eat it

NOVEL COMMANDS

Put the bacon under the chair

Put the hamburger on top of your head

Put the mustard on the chicken

Pour some milk on the hot dog and laugh

UNIT VII   Lesson 68   MEATS AND MISCELLANEOUS

REVIEW COMMANDS

Pick up the bacon and the chicken
Put the ham in the refrigerator; on the table
Put the hot dog next to the hamburger
Put the bun under the tortilla
Put the hot dog in the bun
Take the hot dog out of the bun
Pour the milk into the pitcher
Pour the juice into the glass

COMMANDS

Spread mustard on the hamburger
Put the french fries next to the hamburger
Spread the ketchup on the french fries
Pour the Coke (Pepsi) into the glass
Stir the juice in the glass; cup
Stir the milk in the pitcher
Pour the soup in the bowl; cup; sink

NOVEL COMMANDS

Teacher commands students to combine unusual (zany) mixtures of foods and
add: Sit under the table . . . Put your nose, knees on the table, etc.

UNIT VII   **Lesson 69**   **MEATS AND MISCELLANEOUS**

REVIEW COMMANDS

Stir the soup with a spoon; fork

Spread the ketchup on my bun

Show me the hamburger and the french fries

Give me the chicken and the tortillas

Put the ketchup next to the mustard

Pick up the Coke (Pepsi) and drink it

Spread the mustard on the hot dog

Put the ham in the refrigerator and take it out

COMMANDS

Spread the peanut butter on the bread; bun

Pass me the jam; jelly

Pass the jam to _____ and _____

Pass me the rice

Give me the cracker(s); jam; butter

Spread the butter (jam, jelly) on the cracker

Show me the peanut butter and jelly; rice

Give me a peanut butter (ham, hamburger) sandwich

Pass me the peanut butter and jelly sandwich

NOVEL COMMANDS

Keep making incredible (and inedible) mixtures of foods.

UNIT VII   Lesson 70   FRUITS

REVIEW COMMANDS

Pass me the butter and the crackers
Spread the jam (jelly) on the peanut butter
Point to the rice . . . Touch it and eat it
Pick up the ham (peanut butter) sandwich

COMMANDS

Put the yellow banana on (under) the box of rice
Put the cherries on top of the crackers
Point to the yellow (red, green) apple
Put the green grapes on (next to) the peanut butter
Give me the little strawberries
Pick up the red strawberry . . . Put it in the box
Get the apple (banana, grape) on the table and give it to me; him; her

NOVEL COMMANDS

Get the banana (apple) on my desk and put it under the chair; book; table

Put the cherries and the grapes in a sandwich . . . Sit under the desk and eat the sandwich

UNIT VII   Lesson 71   FRUITS

REVIEW COMMANDS

Draw some strawberries . . . Color them red
Put the yellow banana and the red cherries on the table
Get the grapes and the banana and give them to me
Point to the green grapes and get the green (purple) grapes
Give (student) the red apple and walk around his/her desk

COMMANDS

Show me a lemon . . . Now draw the lemon
Color the lemon yellow and give it to (student)
Cut the oranges on the table and give them to me
Point to the peach . . . Pick up the peach and put it down
Pass me the pear
Put the pear next to the peach
Draw two watermelons
Color the watermelons green and point to them
Draw some oranges
Color the oranges orange and give them to (student)

NOVEL COMMANDS

Color the fruits impossible colors. Ex: Draw a watermelon and color it brown
Jump to the chalkboard with a watermelon on your head

UNIT VII   Lesson 72   FRUITS -- DESSERTS

REVIEW COMMANDS

Show me the oranges and put them on the table; desk ; chair

Color the pear green and the lemon yellow

Point to the peaches and the watermelon

Touch the little (big) peach

Draw two (three, four) bananas and erase them

Get the pear and the grapes and give them to me; him; her

COMMANDS

Give me a cup cake . . . Give a cup cake to (student)

Put the pie on the plate; table

Put the pie in the oven; sink

Spread the ice cream on the cookie

Give her some ice cream . . . Now put it on the cake

Point to the cake . . . Eat the cake

Put the cookie (cup cake, pie, cake) in the oven

Put the cup cake next to the ice cream

NOVEL COMMANDS

Teacher commands students to put the different foods in unusual places in the
kitchen and unexpected rooms of the house . . . Add: smile, laugh, cry, frown,
dance

Stir the mustard and the ketchup . . . Spread them on the ice cream . . . Put the
ice cream on a bun . . . Put them in the oven

UNIT VII   Lesson 73   REVIEW LESSON

(Review in the Unit VIII)

Pour the orange juice in the glass   1.

Stir the cereal and the milk with a spoon   2.

Put the eggs on the table   3.

Put some lettuce on the bread   4.

Put the tomato, the celery, and onion on the lettuce   5.

Show me the salad   6.

Draw a pumpkin and some carrots   7.

Put the beans, the potatoes, and the corn on the plate   8.

Stir the soup in the bowl   9.

Point to the hamburger, the mustard, and the hot dogs   10.

Take the bacon out of the refrigerator   11.

Now give the bacon to me   12.

Show me the chicken on the plate   13.

Show him (her) the french fries and the Coke; Pepsi   14.

Give me a peanut butter sandwich   15.

Put ham on the cracker   16.

Spread the butter on the tortillas   17.

Pick up the peach and the banana   18.

Put the strawberries on the table   19.

Color the grapes purple and the pear green   20.

Get the watermelon and the oranges   21.

Cut the apple with the knife   22.

Put the big pie in the oven . . . Now take it out   23.

Draw some cookies . . . Color the cookies brown   24.

Point to the cup cake and the cake   25.

UNIT VII -- LESSON 73

☒ = Presented   ☒ = Mastered   Date _____

STUDENTS																										
1																										1
2																										2
3																										3
4																										4
5																										5
6																										6
7																										7
8																										8
9																										9
10																										10
11																										11
12																										12
13																										13
14																										14
15																										15
16																										16
17																										17
18																										18
19																										19
20																										20
21																										21
22																										22
23																										23
24																										24
25																										25

TARGET VOCABULARY - UNIT VIII

LESSONS 74 - 84

Space, Order, Position, Number, Time Days of the week

This unit uses the basic concepts taken from the *TEST OF BASIC CONCEPTS* by Ann E. Boehm, Psychological Corporation of America, 1967, 1970.

You will combine these new *ACTIONS* with this new vocabulary.

*These concepts have been introduced in previous units.

Basic Concepts

top	center	
through	as many	
away from	side	
*next to	in front of	
inside	other	
some, not many	alike	
middle	last	
few	never	
farthest	below	
*around	matches	
over	always	
widest	medium sized	
most	*right	
*between	*forward	
whole	zero	
first	above	
nearest	every	
second	separated	
corner	*left	
several	pair	
third	skip	
row	equal	
different	in order	
after	not first or last	
almost	least	
half		

Actions

set (your clock)
will + verb
(future tense)
take

Others

(hour) o'clock
(quarter hour) :15
(half hour) :30
today
Sunday
Monday
Tuesday
Wednesday
Thursday
Friday
Saturday

THIS UNIT REVIEWS CLASSROOM OBJECTS, COLORS, NUMBERS, SHAPES, FOOD AND CLOTHING AND INTRODUCES THE FUTURE TENSE.

BE SURE TO READ EACH LESSON CAREFULLY, AHEAD OF TIME, TO BE PREPARED WITH THE ITEMS YOU WILL NEED.

FEEL FREE TO MAKE AND ADD YOUR OWN RECOMBINATIONS OF THIS AND EARLIER VOCABULARY

UNIT VIII   Lesson 74   BASIC CONCEPTS

Have clocks ready -- or have students make clocks with hands that move.

REVIEW COMMANDS

Pick up two cup cakes and four cookies
Put them down and spread some peanut butter on the cake
Pour me, (*Julio other student*) some milk, orange juice
Drink the milk and pass me the ice cream . . . Give the orange juice
to _____.

COMMANDS

Touch the top of (bottom of) the paper; box; table; chair; book
Walk (skip) through the door
Push the box through the window
Go (run) away from the desk; window; door; table
Show me the box that is away from the table
Put the paper inside the box; desk
Touch your clocks . . . Show me your clock
Set your clock to one o'clock
Set your clock to two (five, one, six, three, four) o'clock

NOVEL COMMANDS

Push your clock and pull it
Put your clock next to your head; nose; ears; eyes, etc.
Put your clock inside your desk
Put your clock on top of your head and set it to four o'clock
Shake your clock and laugh; cry; frown; sing; dance

UNIT VIII   Lesson 75   BASIC CONCEPTS

REVIEW COMMANDS

Pick up the chalk
Put the pencil by the chalk
Put the banana next to the apple
Put three crayons inside the box
Push the chair away from the table
Walk through the door
Show me the top of your head
Point to the bottom of your feet
Set your clock to one (six) o'clock

COMMANDS

Draw a triangle on the blackboard
Draw a circle around the triangle; pencil
Draw a box with two circles around it
Put the book in the middle of the table; chair; desk
Give a few grapes (apples, other fruit) to me; (student)
Throw a few crayons to (student) . . . Catch them, (student)
Walk to the chalkboard farthest from my desk; from (student's) desk
Put some, not many, pencils (pens, crayons) in the box
Show me the crayon farthest from the red (blue, other color) crayon
Write your name and draw a circle around your name
Pick up some, not many, clocks, Kim; (student)
Put down a few clocks and give them to _____
Pick up one clock and set it to seven o'clock
Set your clock to eight (ten, twelve, eleven, nine) o'clock
Put your clock inside your desk

UNIT VIII   Lesson 76   **BASIC CONCEPTS**

REVIEW COMMANDS

Walk around the desk . . . Turn your head

Point to the middle of the room; door; **window**

Give me some (not many) pencils; books

Put a few crayons in the box

Show me the table farthest from the chalkboard; **window; door**

Set your clock to seven o'clock; eight; nine; **ten; eleven; twelve o'clock**

COMMANDS

Take your clock and set it to five o'clock

Show me your clock . . . Now set it to three (twelve) o'clock (**Keep the numbers mixed up**)

Jump over the clock

Show me the widest box; paper

Put your clock between your books

Pick up most of the grapes; cookies; cup **cakes; eggs**

Put the 6 between the 8 and the 5

Put the apple between the banana and the **pear**

Put the red crayon between the blue and the **green**

Give me a whole cup cake; pie; cake

Give me a whole apple . . . Cut the apple

Pick up most of the apples; cherries; grapes; **cookies**

Take your clock and set it to 1:30

Show me your clock

Set your clock to 2:30; (all the half hours to 12:30) (**Keep the numbers mixed up**)

Put your clock inside your desk

UNIT VIII   Lesson 77   BASIC CONCEPTS

REVIEW COMMANDS

Jump over the box
Stand (sit) on the widest paper
Give me most of the crayons
Stand between Ana and (student)
Stand between the two chairs
Show me the whole apple
Set your clock to 2:30; 3:20; 5:30, etc.

COMMANDS

Show me the boy nearest the door
Walk to the chair nearest to you . . . Touch it
Pick up the 1st (2nd, 3rd) ball; pencil; crayon; book, etc.
Sit on the 1st (2nd) chair
Stand on the 3rd chair and smile
Pick up the crayon nearest to the pencils
Show me the corner of the table
Touch the corner of the room; book
Give me several books; pencils; crayons; apples
Look behind me
Stand behind my chair; desk
Put your hands behind you and laugh
Put Juan behind Carlos and Lea behind Juan
Stand in the corner and frown
Take your clock and set it to 2:15
Set your clock to 3:15; 5:15; 10:15, etc.
Set it to 10:15; 6:30; 8:15; 2:30; 3:00; 5:00; 7:30
(Keep mixing up hours, half hours, quarter hours.)

UNIT VIII   Lesson 78   BASIC CONCEPTS

REVIEW COMMANDS

Put your clock in the corner of the room

Put your paper on the corner of your desk

Touch the chair nearest to the window

Put the crayons on the 1st (2nd, 3rd) chair from my desk

Put several pencils behind my head; feet

Set your clock to 6:15; 5:15; 4:15; 10:15; twenty after 2

Put your clock inside your desk

COMMANDS

Pick up your clock and point to it

Set your clock to five after two; ten after one; fifteen after three; twenty after five

Set your clock to almost two o'clock; almost four o'clock; almost six o'clock

(Mix up hours, half hours, 5, 10 & 15 minute intervals)

Touch the chairs in the first row

Put the crayons (pencils, clocks, chairs) in a row

Show me (pick up) the box (book, crayon, ball, block) that is different

Open your eyes

Close your eyes . . . Point to the window after you open your eyes

Open the door and close it

Point to the window after you close the door

Touch the glass (cup, pitcher) that is almost full (empty)

Cut the green (blue, orange, yellow, other colors) paper in half . . . Give me half the paper

Cut the red (green, yellow) apple in half . . . Give me half the apple

Clap your hands after you touch the red apple

UNIT VIII   Lesson 79   **BASIC CONCEPTS**

From this point on, you may give commands in the future tense. (Start with
"You will . . .)

REVIEW COMMANDS

Cut your paper in half

Give me half of the paper

Point to the row of apples; bananas; grapes

Sit down after you touch the book; table; chair

Give me the glass that is almost full; empty

Cut a circle (triangle, paper) in half

Set your clock to 10:00; 11:30; 9:15; 6:00; 8:30; 3:15; 10 **after 5**

COMMANDS

(Teacher now sets clock and says, At _____ you will . . . ,using **future tense**)

At 7 o'clock you will point to the center of your nose

At 6:30 you will draw a circle in the center of your **paper**

At 10 o'clock you will point to the center of the desk; circle

At 8:15 you will give me as many crayons (balls, pencils) **as you have**

Stand on the right (left side of my chair; desk

Put the first ball (book, pencil) in the box

At 20 after 3 you will put the other ball (book, pencil) in the box

At 2:45 you will show me the boy who is in front of Juan

_____ , stand in front of (Maria) (other student)

At 3:15 you will show me who is in front of (Maria) (other student)

Set your clock to 11:30

Give 11:30 To Jose

Give 1:15 To Clara

Put 8:20 under your desk

At 10:30 you will put your clock in front of your chair

At 8:15 you will point to the center of your clock

At 7:25 you will touch the side of your clock

Put your hands in front of your clock

UNIT VIII   Lesson 80   BASIC CONCEPTS

Have flash cards with days of the week written on them. Use cards like this: "Give (card with the name of) Sunday to Alfredo."

REVIEW COMMANDS

Point to the center of the room; box; circle

Jump to the center of the rug

Give me as many pencils as I have

Pick up as many crayons as I have

Put the box on the left (right) side of the table

Put the book in front of the box

Show me the other box; pencil; crayon; paper

Point to the triangle (circle, square) that is different

Put the number 15 in front of 12; six in front of 8, etc.

Set your clock to (any time)

COMMANDS

Show me what you will never touch (fire)

Show me what a baby never has (pair of glasses)

Show me the red apples that are alike

Point to the cookies that are alike

Show me the last chair (boy, girl) in the row

Touch the blouse that matches the skirt

Show me the shirt that matches the pants

Point to the yellow pencil (crayon, chalk) below the desk

Today is Sunday . . . Take it and give Sunday to Alfredo

Pick up Monday . . .Give Monday to Clara

Clara, show me Monday, then throw it to me

Throw Monday to Kim . . . Kim, catch Monday

NOVEL COMMANDS

Sit on Sunday and Monday

Put your nose on Sunday and your knees on Monday

Jump on Monday and laugh and sing

Put Sunday and Monday below the window, etc.

UNIT VIII   Lesson 81   BASIC CONCEPTS

Have ready flash cards for days of the week
Have ready photos of clothes (or picture cards)
Wherever possible, refer to the clothes that students are wearing

REVIEW COMMANDS

Show me the shirts (shoes, pants, socks) that are alike
Point to the boy (girl) who is last; 1st; 2nd; 3rd
Sit below the window
Point to the coat that matches the hat
Show me what a book never has (a tail)
Show me what a hat never has (sleeves)

COMMANDS

Show me what a book always has (sheets)
Point to the medium sized box; banana; orange; apple
Touch the ball (student) on my right (left) side
Walk forward and pick up the blouse; jacket; coat
Walk backward and point forward
Point to the right . . . Point to the left
Give me zero hats; other articles of clothing
Today is Wednesday . . . Point to Wednesday

NOVEL COMMANDS

Put Wednesday on your right ear; shoe
Put Wednesday on your right eye; foot
Pick up Tuesday and put it under your right leg
Put Thursday under your chair; table; clock
Put Tuesday and Thursday on top of (any article of clothing you wish to review)

UNIT VIII   Lesson 82   BASIC CONCEPTS

Use flash cards for days of the week. Ex: "Sit on (card which says) Friday."

Remember, check commands ahead of time, and have appropriate items and/or pictures ready

REVIEW COMMANDS

Pick up Monday (Tuesday, Wednesday) with your right (left) hand

Show me what a foot always has (toes)

Give me a medium sized pencil; crayon; apple; circle; triangle

Push the chair forward; pull the chair backward

Show me the box with zero crayons

Point to Monday and Tuesday with your right hand

Hold Wednesday in your right hand

COMMANDS

Put a clock on every desk . . . Now put it above your head

Point to the clock above your head

Show me the boxes (eggs, beans) that are separated

Point to your left side

Stand on my left (right) side

Show me a pair of black (brown, white) shoes

Show me a pair of shoes that are separated

Point to a pair of stockings; shoes

This is Friday . . . Push your chair forward to Friday

Put Friday to the left of Thursday

Put Thursday to the right of Wednesday

NOVEL COMMANDS

Today is Thursday . . . Take Thursday and Friday and put them below the eggs (shoes, beans, socks) that are separated

Put Wednesday on Friday . . . Put Friday to the right of Thursday

Put Monday to the left of thursday

Put Tuesday under Wednesday

Put Monday on your eyes and Sunday on your head

Give Wednesday and Monday to Juan; Maria

UNIT VIII   Lesson 83   **BASIC CONCEPTS**

REVIEW COMMANDS

Run to the left (right) side of the room
Point to the box above the cupboard; shelf
Give every boy (girl) a crayon; book
Point to the pencils that are separated
Show me the socks that are separated
Point to a black (brown) pair of shoes
Find the red pair of socks
Put Friday to the left of Thursday

COMMANDS

Pick up the paper and draw three lines on it
Skip a line and write your name
Open your book to page 5
Skip a page and show me the next page
Show me the numbers that are equal
Put the boxes in order from small to large
Put the girls (boys) in order from short to tall
Pick up the book that is not first or last
Show me the student that is not first or last
Point to the box with the least (most) crayons; pencils
Pick up the book with the least pages
Point to Saturday
Show me Monday, Tuesday and Thursday
Jorge, take Saturday, Wednesday and Friday and put them behind you
Pick up Sunday . . . Skip Monday and pick up Tuesday
Put Sunday, Monday, Tuesday, Wednesday, etc. in order; in a row

NOTES

UNIT VIII   Lesson **84**   REVIEW LESSON

(Review in the Unit IX)

Set your clock to 7 and 8:30	1.
Set your clock to 5:15 and 10:45	2.
Stand next to the shirt	3.
Put the spoon inside the glass	4.
Pick up some papers	5.
Touch the middle of the circle	6.
Stand between Sunday and Monday	7.
Give me a whole box of crayons	8.
Point to the nearest blouse	9.

(Teacher sets clock and says)

At 5 after 2:00 you will touch the second crayon in the row	10.
At 20 after 3:00 you will put a few crayons on the chair	11.
At 1:15 you will run to the farthest chair	12.
At 4:30 you will walk around the table	13.
At 6;00 you will put your hands over your head	14.
Point to the widest box	15.
Pick up most of the beans	16.
Point to the top of the skirt	17.
Put your arm through the big box; circle; square	18.
Walk away from the chalkboard	19.
Put Tuesday, Wednesday and Thursday in a row	20.
Pick up the triangle that is different	21.
Clap your hands after you touch Friday	22.
Put the jacket in the corner	23.
Pick up several books	24.
Give me zero books	25.
Stand behind me . . . Put your hands above your head	26.
Put Saturday in front of me	27.
Give me Monday, Wednesday and Friday	28.
Skip Tuesday, Thursday and Saturday and pick up Sunday	29.

⊘ = Presented   ⊠ = Mastered   Date _____

STUDENTS

1																						1
2																						2
3																						3
4																						4
5																						5
6																						6
7																						7
8																						8
9																						9
10																						10
11																						11
12																						12
13																						13
14																						14
15																						15
16																						16
17																						17
18																						18
19																						19
20																						20
21																						21
22																						22
23																						23
24																						24
25																						25
26																						26
27																						27
28																						28
29																						29

TARGET VOCABULARY -- UNIT IX

LESSONS 85 - 93

You will combine these new *ACTIONS* with this vocabulary.

Actions	Nouns		Others
pet	cat	deer	by
	kitten	bear	
	dog	tiger	
	puppy	lion	
	butterfly	turtle	
	bird	zebra	
	duck	giraffe	
	chick	elephant	
	rooster	camel	
	hen	snake	
	bee	monkey	
	horse	gorilla	
	pig	hippopotamus	
	sheep	kangaroo	
	cow	eagle	
	turkey	peacock	
	fish	seal	
	rabbit	whale	
	mouse		

Past tense phrases are included in commands in this unit.

Many *basic concepts* (Boehm) are reviewed in this unit.

It will be helpful to have a set of plastic animals and 2 - 3 sets of colored picture cards of the animals listed in the Nouns column.

FEEL FREE TO ADD AND MAKE YOUR OWN RECOMBINATIONS OF VOCABULARY.

UNIT IX   Lesson 85   DOMESTIC ANIMALS

REVIEW COMMANDS

Set the clock to 7:30; 8:15; 10:45 (other times)
At 7:30 you will walk around your desk
At 20 after 5 you will touch the book on (below) the table
At 10:45 you will skip to the nearest window
At 9:05 you will draw a circle in the center of the blackboard

COMMANDS

Point to the little kitten
Point to the big cat
Draw a cat . . . Cut out the cat . . . Color the cat black
Show me a puppy (you drew) in the yard
Draw a dog
Cut out the dog . . . Hold the dog . . . Hold up the dog
Push the dog away from the house . . . Now pet the dog
Point to the dog (you pushed)
Push the puppy next to the dog . . Pet the puppy
Show me the puppy (you pushed)
Hold the cat and the kitten . . . Put them behind the garage
Show me the bird
Pick up the yellow (green, blue) butterfly
Point to the butterfly (you picked up)
Put the bird next to the butterfly (you picked up)

NOVEL COMMANDS

Pretend you are a bird . . . Fly like a bird
Pretend you are a cat and catch the bird
Put the bird on top of (at the bottom of) the house
Jump with the dog
Run with the cat and jump over the fence
Hold up the butterfly and skip away from the garage
Show me the bird
Pick up the yellow (green, blue) butterfly
Point to the butterfly (you picked up)
Put the bird next to the butterfly (you picked up)

UNIT IX   Lesson 86   DOMESTIC ANIMALS

REVIEW COMMANDS

Jump over the puppy
Stand next to the dog
Pick up the kitten and pet it
Draw a cat and pet the cat
Push the bird next the the butterfly
Hold the puppy (kitten) in your arms

COMMAND

Put the duck by the water
Pick up the duck and put it in the water
Point to the rooster and put him on the fence
Touch the chick. . . Rub the little chick's head
Put the chick by the kitten
Show me the hen and hold up the hen
Put the hen by the rooster
Pick up the rabbit. Show me the rabbit you (pushed, petted, rubbed, etc.).
Pet the rabbit; duck; rooster; hen
Point to the bee. . . Touch the bee. . . Put the bee on top of the butterfly

NOVEL COMMANDS

Put the duck and the chick and the rooster in the water. . . Point to the water
and jump
Put the hen under (on) the garage. . . Push the hen into the water
Put the kitten on the rooster's head. . . Put the duck on the kitten's head
Pick up the chick and put it on the duck
Hop backward to the water
Pretend you are a rooster and sing (crow)
Pretend you are a duck and sing (quack)

UNIT IX   Lesson 87   FARM ANIMALS

REVIEW COMMANDS

Pet the bee
Pick up the chick (duck) and hold it up; put it down
Hold the rooster. . . Hold (hold up) the hen
Put the rooster by the hen
Pick up the chick and put it on (inside, under) the box
Put the brown (white) duck by the big black cat
Put the little white chick by the fat white duck
(Use color words + big, little to describe animals)

COMMANDS

Show me the brown (white, black) horse
Touch the little (big) pig
Pick up the little (big) black sheep
Pretend you are a sheep and sing (baa-baa)
Point to the black (white brown) cow
Pass the thin horse and the fat pig to Maria; other student
Put the grey sheep and the fat cow in the yard
Point to the turkey. . . pick up the turkey and pot it down by the cow

NOVEL COMMANDS

Throw the sheep and the cow into the water
Put the little pig on the black cow. . . Put the black cow on your head and pet
the cow
Put the horse and the pig on your arm. . . Put your arm in the water
Put the rabbit under the turkey
Pretend you are a horse and run
Pretend you are a turkey. . Shake your head and sing (gobble, gobble)

UNIT IX   Lesson 88   **FARM ANIMALS**

REVIEW COMMANDS

Pet the fat brown (pink, black) little pig
Point to the big black (white) horse
Put the sheep by the horse (you pointed to)
Show me the black (white, brown) cow
Touch the pig. . . Point to the pig (you touched)
Walk backward to the hen. . . put it on (under) the box
Pass the turkey to _____
Show me the turkey (you passed)

COMMANDS

Touch the fish. . . Put the fish in the water
Pick up the bee and put it on top of the butterfly
Pet the mouse. . . Point to the mouse (you petted)
Throw the fish and the mouse to me
Pick up the rabbit. . . Show me the rabbit (you picked up)
Draw a circle around the fish; bee; rabbit; mouse
Show me the circle (you drew)

NOVEL COMMANDS

Put the bee and the fish on the turkey. . . Put the turkey on your head and
point to your head
Put the mouse on top of your nose and jump backward and forward
Put the fish under the mouse (turkey) and laugh
Put the turkey on your head
Pretend you are a rabbit and eat (mimic nibbling with hands up)

UNIT IX   Lesson 89   ZOO ANIMALS

REVIEW COMMANDS

Pick up the bee. . . Put the bee on top of the bird
Put the mouse in the center of the table; chair
Draw a circle around the mouse
Point to the fish. . . Put it on my foot
Put the bird behind (over, next to, below) the fish

COMMANDS

Point to the turtle. . . Pet the turtle·
Touch the deer. . . Put the deer in the corner
Put the bear to the right of (left of) the rabbit
Show me the deer and put the deer behind the bear
Walk away from the bear and the deer
Pick up the lion and push it forward (pull it backward)
Pick up the tiger and push it backward
Put the tiger in the corner

NOVEL COMMANDS

Put the tiger below the table
Put the deer on my shoulder; head; feet; arms; nose
Put the bear next to your chair; on the table
Put the tigers in a row and laugh and sing
Put (student) behind (2 other students) in a row
Pretend you are a lion and sing (growl)

UNIT IX   Lesson 90   ZOO ANIMALS

REVIEW COMMANDS

Put the deer, bear, and the turtle in a row

Push the tiger away from the fish; turtle

Put the bear behind your head

Give me the bear and jump around the nearest chair

Point to the turtle and put it below the nearest window; desk; table

COMMANDS

Show me the zebra and pass it to the (student)

Touch the elephant and walk away from the elephant

Point to the tall giraffe. . . Draw a pair of giraffes

Pick up the box and put it under the table

Put the snake on the camel

Draw a circle around the snake

Hold the turtle over the snake

(Add past tense commands based on these commands)

NOVEL COMMANDS

Jump around your chair and sit under it

Put the zebra on your shoulders and walk around the table with it

Put a pair of shoes on the zebra

Put the elephant on top of the camel . . Give the camel to (student) and jump around the chair with (student)

Put the snake on the elephant and put them inside the little box. (Let them enjoy the impossibility of this command)

UNIT IX   Lesson 91   ZOO ANIMALS

REVIEW COMMANDS

Point to the snake and put it on the chair
Put the elephant in the corner
Show me the zebra and give it to me
Hold the giraffe over the camel
Pick up the bear and put it below the window
Put the tiger to the right of (left of) the lion
Put the camel behind the giraffe

COMMANDS

Touch the kangaroo and pass the kangaroo to _____
Point to the gorilla and pass it to _____
Draw a triangle around the gorilla
Show me the monkey and put the monkey, the gorilla and the kangaroo in a row
Point to the hippopotamus and draw a big circle around it
Show me the hippopotamus and pass it to _____

NOVEL COMMANDS

(Keep putting different combinations of animals near, above, below, next to others)
Hold up the hippopotamus and put it on your feet; nose, etc.
Pet the gorilla and the monkey
Jump with the kangaroo around the room
Pretend you are a gorilla (Show a frightening pose with arms up high)
Shake the hippopotamus

UNIT IX   Lesson 92   ZOO ANIMALS

REVIEW COMMANDS

Point to the monkey and put it below (above, next to, to the right of, to the left of) the hippopotamus

Show me a few elephants; zebras; camels; gorillas

Point to the tigers (lions) that are separated

Pick up the bear (kangaroo) and put it in the corner

COMMANDS

Touch the eagle. . . Show me the eagle. . . Show me the eagle (you touched)

Hold up the eagle. . . Point to the eagle (you held up)

Show me the peacock

Draw a circle around the peacock

Show me the circle (you drew around the peacock)

Touch the black seal and push it into the water

Point to the whale

Put the whale in the water

Show me the whale (you put in the water)

NOVEL COMMANDS

Pretend you are a peacock and walk around the room (strut proudly and slowly) (Add yours and the students' zany commands)

Notes

UNIT IX   Lesson 93   REVIEW LESSON

(Review in Unit X)

Point to the dog and put it in the corner   1.

Hold up the kitten and the duck   2.

Put the kitten inside the box   3.

Draw three cats in a row   4.

Show me a little puppy. . . Pet the puppy   5.

Put the rooster on the desk farthest from the door   6.

Put the horse below the window   7.

Show me the hen, the cow, and the chick   8.

Pick up the sheep and the pig   9.

Put the bird between the butterfly and the bee   10.

Give me the turkey and the rabbit   11.

Show me several fish   12.

Point to the fish that is different   13.

Draw a circle around the snake and the mouse   14.

Put the turtle by the water   15.

Put the tiger, the deer, and the lion in a row   16.

Put the seal to the left of the whale   17.

Put the eagle under the table   18.

Put the fish and the seal in the water   19.

Touch the big peacock and the big whale   20.

Pass me the brown bear   21.

Show me the tall giraffe and the grey elephant   22.

Put the camel and the rabbit next to the zebra   23.

Push the monkey and the gorilla forward   24.

Put the kangaroo to the right of the hippopotamus   25.

◹ = Presented ☒ = Mastered Date _____

STUDENTS

	1	2	3	4	5	6	7	8	9	10	11	12	13	14	15	16	17	18	19	20		
1																						1
2																						2
3																						3
4																						4
5																						5
6																						6
7																						7
8																						8
9																						9
10																						10
11																						11
12																						12
13																						13
14																						14
15																						15
16																						16
17																						17
18																						18
19																						19
20																						20
21																						21
22																						22
23																						23
24																						24
25																						25

TARGET VOCABULARY -- UNIT X

LESSONS 94 - 102

You will combine these new *ACTIONS* with this vocabulary.

Actions	Nouns		Others
be	doctor	cook	as
drive	dentist	waiter/	thank you
tap	druggist/	waitress	while
strum	pharmacist	menu	
play	aspirin	baker	
	clerk	butcher	
	nurse	barber	
	money	beautician	
	plumber	bus driver	
	carpenter	pilot	
	electrician	tickets	
	mechanic	telephone	
	gardener	operator	
	fireman (woman)	dial	
	mailman (woman)	truck driver	
	policeman (woman)	musician	
	motorcycle	drum	
		guitar	
		piano	
		dancer	
		airplane	
		spaceship	

FEEL FREE TO ADD AND MAKE YOUR OWN RECOMBINATIONS OF NEW AND EARLIER VOCABULARY.

RECORD THE NOVEL COMMANDS THAT YOUR STUDENTS HAVE CREATED

UNIT X   LESSON 94   OCCUPATIONS

NOTE: Use costumes, accessories, or props that will help the students 'be' the various workers. Remember to put commands in the past and future tenses as well.

REVIEW COMMANDS

Put the seal to the left (right) of the whale

Point to the tall giraffe and the grey elephant

Skip forward to the kangaroo

Put three (two, four) tigers in a row

Show me the whale (you put in the water)

COMMANDS

Show me the doctor . . . Pick up the doctor and put him down

Point to the dentist . . . Kim; pretend you are the dentist . . . Look into Thieu's mouth and touch his teeth

Touch the druggist/pharmacist

Put the dentist by the druggist

Put the doctor (druggist) by the window; table; chair

Lucy, be the doctor . . . Touch Sarah's head and give her some aspirin

Show me the clerk; nurse

Put the clerk behind the table

Rosa, be a clerk . . . Show a blouse and skirt to Maria . . . Maria give her some money

Put a cup of water next to the nurse

Draw a circle around the nurse

Show me some money

Pick up the money and give it to me . . . Thank you . . . Now give the money to the policeman

NOVEL COMMANDS

Give a hot dog to the doctor; dentist

(Command students to give food or household items to the various workers. Add: jump backward, skip around, hop forward, etc. Also add: frown, smile, laugh dance.)

UNIT X   LESSON 95   OCCUPATIONS

REVIEW COMMANDS

Put the druggist next to the clerk
Color the druggist; pharmacist
Pass me some aspirin
Put the doctor by the nurse
Hug the doctor and the dentist
Give the orange juice to the doctor
Give the money to the clerk
Give the aspirin to the nurse

COMMANDS

Point to the plumber
Show the toilet to the plumber
Juan, be a plumber . . . Look at the toilet and frown
Pick up the carpenter
Give the hammer (nails) to the carpenter
Sara, be a carpenter . . . Hit the nail with the hammer
Show me the electrician . . . Show the lamp to the electrician
Pick up (put down) the mechanic
Show the T. V. to the mechanic
Clara, be a mechanic . . . Touch the T. V. and frown
Put the mechanic by the gardener
Give the hose (rake, shovel) to the gardener

UNIT X   LESSON 96   OCCUPATIONS

NOTE: Collect any costumes or accessories that would make the students
          'become' the listed community helpers.

REVIEW COMMANDS

Show me the carpenter . . . Put him (her) by the plumber

Put the plumber by the electrician

Put the electrician by the light

Open and close the door

Knock on the door

Point to the mechanic and give him to me

Pick up the gardener and give the hose (rake) to the gardener

COMMANDS

Pick up the fireman; woman . . . Show me the fireman; woman

Be a fireman; woman . . . Pour some water on the fire

Show me the mailman; woman

Juan, be a mailman . . . Juan, give me some letters

Touch the garbage collector/trash collector

Show the trash collector to (student)

Give the garbage can to the garbage collector

Show me the milkman

Point to the policeman; woman

Karen, be a policewoman

Sal, give the paper to the policewoman

_____, be a policeman and blow your whistle

Point to the motorcycle

Put the policeman on his motorcycle

UNIT X   LESSON 97   OCCUPATIONS

REVIEW COMMANDS

Pretend you are a garbage collector and pick up the garbage

Be a milkman and give me some milk

Show me the policeman; woman

Put the policewoman between the milkman and the fireman; woman

Put the policeman on the motorcycle

COMMANDS

Point to the cook and the waitress; waiter

Touch the cook . . . Put the cook by the oven

Knock on the oven . . . Open and close the oven door

Touch the menu

Show me the waitress . . . Give the plate (menu) to the waitress; waiter

Be a waiter, Juan . . . Give the coffee to Kim . . . Kim, drink the coffee and smile

Show me the baker . . . Pass the bread to the baker

Tami, be a baker . . . Put the bread in the oven

Clara, pretend you are a butcher . . . Cut up the meat and hang it up . . . Hold it up and smile . . . Show the meat to the cook

Sara, pretend you are the cook . . . Look at the meat, cut it, touch it and frown

Pretend you are a barber and cut _____'s hair

Put the barber by the beautician

Pretend you are a beautician . . . Comb Maria's hair

UNIT X   LESSON 98   OCCUPATIONS

REVIEW COMMANDS

Put the meat between the butcher and the cook
Pass the bread to the baker
Show me the waitress and the menu
Point to the barber
Touch the beautician
Rub the barber's head
Run with the baker
Give the money to the butcher

COMMANDS

Pick up the bus driver and put him (her) down
Give some money to the bus driver
Hold up the truck driver
Show the tickets to the bus driver; truck driver
Pick up the telephone operator and her telephone
Sara, be a telephone operator and dial (pick up) your telephone
Point to the truck driver
Skip backward with the truck driver and the telephone operator
Jerry, be a truck (bus) driver and drive your truck; bus (make motions of driving

NOVEL COMMANDS

Rub the barber's head on the baker's feet
Jump backward with the truck driver
Skip around the truck driver and laugh
Rub your head on the telephone operator's telephone
Run to the bus driver, hug him and give him a ticket

UNIT X   LESSON 99   OCCUPATIONS

REVIEW COMMANDS

Run to the telephone operator and the truck driver
Jump with the bus driver
Give me the bus driver
Show me the ticket and the money
Drive your truck; bus

COMMANDS

Touch the painter . . . Hold up the painter
Pick up the painter's hat; jacket
Show me an astronaut
Point to the astronaut's shoes; gloves; arms; legs, etc.
Give the banker to (student); me
_____, be a banker and give me some money
Point to the banker (who gave me the money)
Pick up the farmer
Show me the farmer's shirt; overalls; hat
Be a farmer and sit on your tractor
Drive your tractor around the field
Show me the farmer (who drove his tractor around the field)

NOVEL COMMANDS

Push the tractor around the farmer
Sit under the tractor and frown
Put the farmer's overalls on the banker
Give the banker's money to the painter

UNIT X   LESSON 100   OCCUPATIONS

REVIEW COMMANDS

Be an astronaut and point up and jump
Show me the astronaut (who pointed and jumped)
Give some money to the banker
Put a rake and a hose next to the farmer
Walk away from the painter

COMMANDS

Point to the musician . . . Touch the musician
Show me the drum; guitar
Tap the drum and the guitar . . . Hold them up and put them down
Tap the guitar . . . Strum the guitar
Hold the drum in your right (left) hand
Strum the guitar with your right hand
Show me the piano
Be a musician and play the piano . . . Strum the guitar . . . Tap the drum
Hold the guitar in your right hand and the drum in your left hand

UNIT X   LESSON 101   OCCUPATIONS

REVIEW COMMANDS

Show me the musician and his guitar; drum; piano
Pick up the drum and hold it up
Tap the drum and strum the guitar
Walk to the piano and play it

COMMANDS

Walk with the musician to the dancer
Jorge, be a dancer . . . Dance with _____
Now dance with me
While Jorge dances, play the guitar; piano; drum
Point to the pilot . . . Touch the airplane
Put the pilot in the airplane
Pick up the pilot and put him next to the astronaut
Touch the spaceship . . . Put the astronaut in the spaceship
Show me the bit (little) airplane
Put the big airplane, the little airplane and the spaceship in a row
Walk with the pilot to his airplane
Hop with the astronaut to his spaceship

Notes

UNIT X   LESSON 102   REVIEW LESSON

Put the policeman (woman) on his (her) motorcycle	1.
Point to the fireman (woman) and the hose	2.
Pick up the mailman . . . Pick up his letters	3.
Show me the garbage collector	4.
Touch the milkman and the telephone operator	5.
Give the doctor an aspirin	6.
Put the dentist and the pharmacist under the desk	7.
Give the beautician some money	8.
Put the carpenter next to the electrician	9.
Put the plumber, the gardener, and the mechanic in a row	10.
Show me the cook, the waitress, and the menu	11.
Comb the barber's hair	12.
Point to the pilot and the airplane	13.
Pick up the butcher and put him down	14.
Give the bus driver (truck driver) a ticket	15.
Push the astronaut to his spaceship	16.
Put the guitar next to the musician	17.
Pick up the painter and put him down	18.
Pull the farmer to his tractor	19.
Put the money next to the clerk	20.
Show me the dancer and the guitar	21.
Pick up some money and give it to the banker	22.
Point to the telephone operator	23.
Dial the telephone	24.
Be a policeman . . . Hold up your hand and blow your whistle	25.

UNIT X -- LESSON 102

☑ = Presented   ☒ = Mastered   Date _____

STUDENTS

1																				1
2																				2
3																				3
4																				4
5																				5
6																				6
7																				7
8																				8
9																				9
10																				10
11																				11
12																				12
13																				13
14																				14
15																				15
16																				16
17																				17
18																				18
19																				19
20																				20
21																				21
22																				22
23																				23
24																				24
25																				25

Other Excellent ESL Materials--Resource Guide

__We Learn English Through Action__ is the Student Book which accompanies __Teaching English Through Action.__

It has already proven most successful for Grades 3-12 and for adults.

It guarantees that all the material covered in Listening Comprehension is now used for Speaking, Reading, and Writing.

__Teaching English Through Action__ contains samples and guide lines for how to use __We Learn English Through Action__

Testing for __Teaching English Through Action__

CONTINUUM---TESTING

FOR THE CUM FOLDER, TEACHER, ADMINISTRATOR, AND PARENT INFORMATION

Packet of 25 cards. One card for each student.

Each 2 sided card (11" x 17") contains ALL the Tests from __Teaching English Through Action.__

(Applies to Spanish, French, and German versions, too.)

For recording test results in Listening, Speaking, Reading, and Writing

L: Listening
S: Speaking
R: Reading
W: Writing

_____ SCHOOL
ESL/FOREIGN LANGUAGE
Student Profile . . . Continuum
Teaching Language Through Action (T.P.R.) --**B.Segal Cook**
I.S.B.N. 0-938395 01 - 7

◌ : Introduced
⊠ : Mastery

Name_____ Grade _____ Teacher _____

__Teaching ESL/Foreign Language - Speaking, Reading, and Writing__

Teaching Foreign Language

or _____

Teaching English as a Second Language

SPEAKING

READING

WRITING

Bertha E. Segal Cook

Level 2

• **Compiled by Berty Segal Cook**

*Contains a guided speaking program that is highly motivating and successful.

*Samples of **NATURAL APPROACH** reading activities in English(ESL book) Reading activities in Spanish, French, German, and Japanese (F.L. book)

*Samples of transfer from Imperative to Present, Past, and Future Tenses

*When to Introduce Grammar

*28 Writing Activities

*Sample Tests--level 1 and 2

*Contains many examples of early and intermediate reading and writing experiences

Teaching English Through Action

Teaching English Through Action is a comprehensive guide of daily lesson plans implementing the Total Physical Response (T.P.R.) Approach to English as a Second Language. It is an excellent tool for teaching beginning and intermediate students of ANY age level.

It ha ten units which contain the essential vocabulary needed for survival and success in English

Each unit contains:

1. TARGET VOCABULARY---This is an overview of the words which will be taught <u>via commands</u> in the succeeding group of lessons.

2. INDIVIDUAL LESSON PLANS--a step-by-step detailing of <u>exactly what commands</u> are to be presented. T.P.R. is a euphoric experience for both teachers and students, and it is very necessary to have very well planned commands at your fingertips in order to remain " in command of the situation" (Pardon the pun.)

With these specific directions you will have control as well as enjoyment.

3. REVIEW LESSON--This is a review of the vocabulary of the entire unit. This lesson should be given orally.

4. RECORD OF MASTERY---There is a grid for recording mastery (or need for further review) with each Review Lesson. It can serve as:

   *a small group(pull out) grid
   *a large group(entire class) grid

This provides a record of each student's progress and will be helpful to teachers and resource teachers in reporting to parents, principal, aide, etc.

Bertha (Berty) Segal Cook is rated one of the top ESL/ Foreign Language teacher trainers in the nation.
She has served as a County ESL teacher trainer, a district resource specialist, and a classroom teacher. She is the author of several highly practical teaching guides. Among the best known is Teaching English Through Action (also in Spanish, French, German, Japanese, Russian, Sepwepemc, St'at'imcets, Inupiak Daketh (Carrier) and Chilcotin

Berty Segal, Inc.
1749 E. Eucalyptus St.
Brea, CA. 92821
http://www.tprsource.com
Email bertysegal;@sbcglobal.net

500- 5- 05   I.S.B.N. 0-938395-35-1

Mr. Joseph E. Leaf
ESL Coordinator
Norristown Area School District

Mr. Joseph E. Leaf
ESL Coordinator
Norristown Area School District

Teaching English Through Action

Teaching English Through Action is a comprehensive guide of daily lesson plans implementing the Total Physical Response (T.P.R.) Approach to English as a Second Language. It is an excellent tool for teaching beginning and intermediate students of ANY age level.

It ha ten units which contain the essential vocabulary needed for survival and success in English Each unit contains:

1. TARGET VOCABULARY---This is an overview of the words which will be taught <u>via commands</u> in the succeeding group of lessons.

2. INDIVIDUAL LESSON PLANS--a step-by-step detailing of <u>exactly what commands</u> are to be presented. T.P.R. is a euphoric experience for both teachers and students, and it is very necessary to have very well planned commands at your fingertips in order to remain " in command of the situation" (Pardon the pun.)

With these specific directions you will have control as well as enjoyment.

3. REVIEW LESSON--This is a review of the vocabulary of the entire unit. This lesson should be given orally.

4. RECORD OF MASTERY---There is a grid for recording mastery (or need for further review) with each Review Lesson. It can serve as:

   *a small group(pull out) grid
   *a large group(entire class) grid

This provides a record of each student's progress and will be helpful to teachers and resource teachers in reporting to parents, principal, aide, etc.

Bertha (Berty) Segal Cook is rated one of the top ESL/ Foreign Language teacher trainers in the nation. She has served as a County ESL teacher trainer, a district resource specialist, and a classroom teacher. She is the author of several highly practical teaching guides. Among the best known is Teaching English Through Action (also in Spanish, French, German, Japanese, Russian, Sepwepemc, St'at'imcets, Inupiak Daketh (Carrier) and Chilcotin

Berty Segal, Inc.
1749 E. Eucalyptus St.
Brea, CA. 92821
http://www.tprsource.com
Email bertysegal;@sbcglobal.net

500- 5- 05   I.S.B.N. 0-938395-35-1